THE QUESTIONS MEN ASK

By the same author:

Time to Share
Manhunt
The Christian Man

The Questions Men Ask

JIM SMITH

KINGSWAY PUBLICATIONS

EASTBOURNE

Printed in Great Britain for
KINGSWAY PUBLICATIONS LTD
Lottbridge Drove, Eastbourne, E. Sussex BN23 6NT by
Richard Clay Ltd, Bungay, Suffolk.
Typeset by Nuprint Ltd, Harpenden, Herts AL5 4SE.

I dedicate this book
to Alan.
With thanks for his friendship and support
both to me, and to my family.

Contents

INTRODUCTION

Questions, Questions, Questions

After fifteen years of marriage, Mary and I were very happy with our three children—David, who was thirteen, John eleven, and Paul four.

Then, to our delight, we found that we were expecting a fourth child. We were all very excited, especially Paul, who kept feeling his new brother/sister in Mummy's tum.

Children never stop asking questions, and this led Paul to ask me *the* question when we were out walking together. He was happily chatting away, and I was thinking of other things, when through my thoughts came an insistent tug on my hand, and, 'Well, Daddy?'

'Well what?' I asked, in all innocence.

'Where do babies come from, Daddy?'

I'm quite good with words, but I had an ominous feeling that I was in for a bad time. So as breezily as I could, I replied, 'Well, babies come from Mummy's tummy. They grow there, where they are safe and warm, and then when they're ready, they are born. Now—shall we go to the swings?'

But he was not to be denied.

'Daddy, how did that baby get into Mummy's tummy?'

I'll spare you the rest, but needless to say I got acutely embarrassed, totally tied up in knots, and wished that I were somewhere else. I know that as a modern parent, I should have been able to tell him all the facts without blushing, but somehow it didn't work out that way.

Incidentally, my attempts to explain conception and birth were obviously totally inadequate. Stephen was born by Caesarean section, and as soon as I could, I took Paul to see him. Paul was really thrilled, and when we went to see Mary in the ward, he couldn't stop talking about it. But as we prepared to leave, he said, 'Mummy, before we go, can I feel the baby in your tummy?'

As we grow older, we never lose this questioning mind. In fact the human race has made many of its most significant advances on the strength of it. Some of the issues we face have been, and still are, very complex—like where do babies come from! But we've still questioned and enquired, until we have gained some understanding.

This questioning mind isn't an accident, but is one of our God-given instincts. God doesn't want to be followed by robots, and often reveals himself through and because of our questions.

One man in the Bible put his feelings like this: 'I devoted myself to knowledge and study; I was determined to find wisdom, and the answers to my questions, and to learn how wicked and foolish stupidity is' (Ecclesiastes 7:25).

Yet even though we have been equipped with minds like this, many men don't seem to want to put them to work on the hard and nagging questions of daily living.

One of the reasons for this is that we've learned the dubious art of living our lives in separate compartments, and we do not allow what happens in one part to affect the others. So while we might bring our enquiring minds to bear on a problem at work, or with the car, we don't bring the same mind into the very different compartments of our marriage, our family, our personal standards, and the more difficult and unresolvable problems at work.

This breaking of our lives into compartments might seem attractive on the surface, but it denies our essential nature, and makes us much less fun to live with. We are meant to face the hard and difficult questions about ourselves and our circumstances—although doing so with an open and honest mind is a hard option for us. But it does lead us into truth— the truth about life, ourselves, our wives and families, our hopes and fears, our God. Over the years, as I have worked with and among men, I've heard certain questions again and again. These are the questions to be found in this book.

I would encourage you to start with the questions that seem most relevant to you, rather than read every page. I haven't got all the answers, but I hope that the things I have written will start you thinking, and searching for truth yourself. The last section is devoted to questions about God. Please look at those pages with special interest and care, for I believe that we men can only discover the answers to our questions when we've faced him for ourselves.

SECTION ONE

Personal

Can I be successful?

One of England's top football club chairmen appeared on TV recently, and was asked what he found attractive about the job. He replied quite simply: 'I like success.'

I'm sure he speaks for most men, whatever they do, because we all want success. Why? Being successful gives us:

* Money and possessions
* Power and influence
* Achievement and a sense of fulfilment

We can hold our heads high in the presence of other men, and live with a greater sense of security. We may have to face failure in our lives, but we don't set out to find it. We want success, and all the benefits that go with it.

The Bible is not against material success, prosperity, fulfilment or achievement. Some of the men described there achieved great wealth, power and influence, and still remained right with God and men. They weren't corrupted or spoilt by their success.

But many are corrupted by success, or find its price a very high one. Some successful people finish up living lonely, friendless and disillusioned lives. There are perils in success, and the Bible explains them very clearly:

* The desire for success can drive those who have it to bad and even evil behaviour.
* Success can lead us to believe that we are secure. This is a dangerous misconception, as many a redundant man can testify.
* We have spiritual needs as men, and these need to be faced

16

and met. Worldly success can hide these needs from us, so that when called to account for our lives, we will be found unprepared. Jesus told a story about a very successful farmer who did just this, and his conclusion needs to be taken to heart:

> You fool! This very night you will have to give up your life; then who will get all these things you have kept for yourself?... This is how it is with those who pile up riches for themselves but are not rich in God's sight (Luke 12:20–21).

It is possible to be successful without any reference to God, and without sacrificing one's morals or convictions. But it is equally possible—and much more satisfying—to be successful and stay within God's laws.

Put God first in all things

Those who already believe in God need to lay all their ambitions and desires before him in an open and honest way. Then God will indicate which things he approves of, and which are out of line with his purposes. God does want to help us in this way. Those who have never thought of bringing their success under God's scrutiny might like to look at the last section of this book, to see what he's really like and what he expects of those who serve him.

In whatever state be content

The true test of Christian success is how we feel about things when they don't seem to work out. Are you able to be content in whatever state you find yourself—great success and achievement, or apparent disaster?

Do not see success as a personal possession

For the Christian man, all success, of whatever type, is for the glory of God, and for his use to extend his work. Do you give him thanks for all he's achieving through your life? Is he able to use what he has given you for the sake of others?

Why do I find it hard to say how I feel?

I was at a conference recently, and was feeling very low. One of our children died shortly after birth a few years ago, and every now and again, it all gets on top of me. I longed to talk about how I was feeling that day, and there were people there whom I could talk to, but I just couldn't do it. I kept putting it off.

Have you ever had the experience of wanting to talk about very personal things, but not being able to find the courage?

After thirty-eight years of life, I still find it very hard to say how I'm feeling. Sometimes I hide my feelings because I've been hurt. Then I bury them so deep, that no one can get at them. I determine that no one will see how I'm feeling, and I bristle like a porcupine, snapping at anyone who tries to help me. Sometimes I'm almost crying inside for someone to help, to listen, or to share, but I'm so trapped behind the male image, that I struggle on.

It isn't always painful feelings that cause problems. I've even found it hard to say 'thank you' sometimes when people offer compliments or gifts. In my embarrassment I say the wrong thing, regret it, and then retreat behind my wall.

Why have I and countless other men got into this state with our feelings?

* We've forgotten how to show our feelings.
* Showing our feelings leaves us open to being hurt, so we hide them.
* A bad experience in the past stops us wanting to try again.
* We're afraid we'll look ridiculous.
* We're afraid others will offer us pity.
* We don't believe anyone else feels the same.

* We believe expressing feelings is for women.

Human beings are 'feeling' orientated, yet we're trying to live as though we're not. No wonder we get into such a muddle. We believe that hiding our feelings is strength, whereas it's weakness. The man who is honest about his feelings is the strong one. He gets the help he needs, and is able to come to terms with himself.

So how can you live in order to express your feelings more?

Be honest with yourself

God gave men feelings—they are an essential part of life. Start facing the truth about yourself—it will make you a much more satisfied person.

Start considering others

A good way to begin to experience your own feelings is to start considering the feelings and needs of others. This will cause your own feelings to come alive.

Explore your feelings

Instead of trying to be hard, examine how you feel about certain experiences. Were you encouraged, hurt, puzzled, sad, happy?

Show your feelings

Where you can, take the chance to show how you feel. Accept a compliment with joy, share a doubt or sadness. Start with small things, and see where it leads.

Share your feelings

This experience is the real one for men who want to discover their feelings again. Share with your wife, or a close friend. It's very risky, and takes time, patience and understanding. It's a big challenge—but men like a challenge. Why shrink away from this one?

Can God forgive any sin?

Open any newspaper, or watch any TV news programme, and we soon become aware of the awful things that men are capable of doing. We're shocked by what we read or see—the murders, rapes, oppression, crime, greed, anger, evil and sin. Yet if we're honest, most of us know that we're far from perfect inside, and that we're all capable of doing or thinking evil things. Men have great potential, but we are also very carnal.

It's this feeling of imperfection that keeps many men from church. For all our faults, we are not hypocrites. Somehow we sense that God would not have these dark places in us; that we cannot come to him unless we do something about them. Consequently many men never hear how God really feels, and have to lead their lives condemned by their sins. There is no escape from the wrongs of the past.

How does God react to these evils within us? He has made his position quite clear.

No one is beyond his love

One of the most astonishing things about God is that no one is beyond his love. Christ appealed to the religious, the secular and the criminal, and each found that he cared for them, even when he regretted their sin.

No one can clean himself up

God loves, but he doesn't close his eyes to the sin and evil in us, or the offence that it causes him. There's nothing we can do about it. We might be tempted to think that we can clean ourselves up a bit, so that we look presentable to God, but it can't be done, because he sees to the very bottom of our lives. If we're honest we know this is true.

God wants to clean us up

No matter what we've done, or however low we have sunk, the desire in the heart of God is for forgiveness and healing. He doesn't just want to offer a second chance, he wants to make us new people. This is God's statement of intent: 'For Christ died for sins once for all, the righteous for the unrighteous, to bring you to God' (1 Peter 3:18, New International Version).

God has acted on his promise

God has taken action to make the new start possible. On the cross, Jesus paid the price for all sin. It's so easy to write, but much harder to imagine. I once counselled a girl who had been raped, and I said this to her: 'You have to believe that it is as if all the evil of that experience was endured by Jesus on the cross. It is as if he was raped for you, so that you can start to live again.'

God does not want us to be condemned. His desire is that we should be convicted of our sin and come to him for forgiveness. No matter what you have done, God can forgive you.

God can forgive any sin.

Will my income be enough?

My eldest son came down to breakfast this week with a worried look on his face. He wanted to go to the theatre with his school, and buy a new shirt. No matter how much he tried to work out his money, he could not afford both. The only help I could give was to point out to him that he was facing one of the great masculine problems of life—too many demands on not enough money. I'm still waiting to see how he resolves it—I might learn something!

Some men earn so much money that they've no need to be concerned about whether they have enough. But most of us have to face the pressures of finance—too many demands and not enough money—daily. This so easily brings stress and worry. This is particularly so in a society which values material possessions highly, constantly bombards us with new products on television, and offers apparently 'easy credit'.

Money is a necessary part of life, but it doesn't need to become a worry. How can we live so that it isn't?

Keep it in perspective

Money is necessary, but other things are more important, such as health, family, relaxation and a sense of purpose. Keeping these things in the front of our minds will keep money in its right place.

Know the difference between needs and wants

We come under pressure when we confuse wants and needs. Do you mix them, or separate them?

Have a sense of humour

Advertisements should make us laugh! They're trying to get us to live beyond our income. Don't be tricked by them.

Beware credit

Before signing a credit agreement, read the small print, and work out the real price. Credit takes a long time to pay back, and in the end the goods bought have often lost their sparkle, and have become a millstone.

Be disciplined

Mary and I pay for the extras with cash. This stops us buying on impulse. We all need some controls on spending. How do you discipline yourself?

Mary and I are learning to rely more and more on God to provide for us, and this is such a joy. He has never failed to provide the necessities of life, and occasionally some of the luxuries as well. It's a radically different approach to living in the financial rat race. Have you ever thought of giving God a chance to provide for you?

How can I handle stress?

A hundred years ago, the minister of my local Parish Church would take a whole day to conduct a funeral. Today, he would think nothing of doing two or even three in an afternoon. This is a sharp reminder of how much the pace of life has quickened in the last hundred years. This same increase has come to all walks of life. All of us—men and women, old and young—are living very fast lives. It's not surprising that under these pressures we get stressed. Stress is not a crime, nor is it a mental weakness.

Some of its causes are:

* Changes in lifestyle: getting married, having a baby, moving house, losing a loved one, a new job, retirement, redundancy, illness, depression, financial difficulties and so on.
* Conflict; in relationships, jobs and expectations.
* Feeling out of control of a situation—that there's nothing we can do about our circumstances.

Stress in one area of our life will affect all of our life. Problems at work, for example, will put stress on our marriage. There's no easy solution to living with stress, but there are some areas that, with thought, can become less stressful and more creative.

Escape routes

Are there ways you can escape from the stressful situation, if only for a short time, like taking a walk, visiting the club, reading a book or practising a hobby? These escape routes provide you with a chance to cool down and retain a balance.

Identify and adjust

Some of the causes of stress are obvious if we will only take time to identify them. Excessive hours at work, financial over-commitment, too high expectations, too ambitious a lifestyle, inadequate rest and relaxation, insufficient time with the family, non-acceptance of situations that can't be changed. It's worth spending time identifying stress points, and taking the appropriate action. The cost of not doing so could be very high.

Examine lifestyle

Is your way of life causing unnecessary stress? Some people live too fast and expect too much. In general, simplifying lifestyle lowers stress levels.

Don't compare

Each of us can stand different levels of stress. If we compare ourselves with other people, we're bound to finish up feeling bad, and this causes more stress! Find out what you can stand, and then check yourself against that measure.

You're valuable

I've learnt that I'm precious to God, regardless of what I achieve, or how busy my life becomes. He loves me the way I am, and has a perfect plan for my life. I'm learning to relax into that plan and this has lowered my stress level, and has enabled me to achieve more by doing less. Perhaps this is a path that you should explore.

Release it

Stress builds up inside us, like a river trapped behind a dam. Releasing the river eases the pressures. Personally, I like to run, travel and spend time with my family, either playing football in the park, or just talking and walking. These are the ways that I release the stress 'dam'. What do you do? Most of all, I find that pressures are eased as I share them with my wife. Do you share them with your wife, or are you bottling them all up inside?

Can I be a better person?

This is the third book that I've written for men in the last four years. To do this I've had to talk to a lot of men, and to take a very honest look at them and at myself. I've come to the conclusion that while we are capable of truly great things, we're also capable of very low and deceitful things as well. On the inside, we're not of the highest quality.

Sometimes I give myself high marks as a person. Last Sunday Mary wasn't well, so I got the children up and out to church so that she could rest. In the past, I would have made her get up, but I'm learning to be more considerate. I want to be more helpful, considerate and understanding, and with great effort I can achieve these standards for a while. I want to control my temper, my language and my thoughts, I want to stop being self-centred, self-seeking, arrogant and proud, and I make a real effort to do so. But then it all goes wrong. Something happens, and a darker person seems to emerge from inside me, shocking me by his low behaviour, his small mindedness, his arrogance, pride and filth.

One of the reasons why I trust Christ is that he made it clear that he knows all about the real me when he said:

> It is what comes out of a person that makes him unclean. For from the inside, from a person's heart, come the evil ideas which lead him to do immoral things, to rob, kill, commit adultery, be greedy, and do all sorts of evil things; deceit, indecency, jealousy, slander, pride, and folly—all these evil things come from inside a person and make him unclean (Luke 7:20–23).

What he says seems so right. I find these things inside myself and they defeat all my efforts to be a better man. How do you feel about them?

There are many in the world today who advocate self-help and self-improvement. They seem sincere people, and nothing would please me more than to believe that through our own efforts the quality of men could be improved. But for all their conviction, these people do not take the true state of the masculine heart into account, and so their efforts are to no avail. They're putting sticking plaster on a wound that needs surgery. Are you falling into their trap?

Only God takes the true state of the male heart into account, offering the viable alternative to self-help. He offers drastic surgery—a clean heart and a new start to those who follow Christ. He is able to sort us out from the inside. Some men think that this is a soft option, but they couldn't be more wrong. It takes courage to recognize the darkness inside, it takes courage to surrender to God, and it takes courage to follow his very tough ways. But those who find this courage discover a God who can change them from the inside and who can even use frailty and weakness, as well as utilizing strength.

You can try to be a better person yourself, or you can recognize the truth and come to God. Is it time to choose?

Can I face failure?

Most of us are afraid of failure. The manager of a top English football club put it like this recently: 'Every time we play a match, I wonder whether we will lose. I feel a bit frightened of failure.' Another top sportsman, facing a series of defeats, says, 'No one likes a whitewash.'

We don't like failure, because in a society which places such high value on success, failure leaves us on the outside. We feel rejected and hurt, and we have to suffer alone, suppressing our pain, and hoping that there might be something better round the corner.

However much we might not like it, failure is a part of our experience, and we have to develop some way of living with it in every part of our lives—work, marriage, family and personal. So rather than asking the question, 'Can I live with failure?', it's much more useful to ask, 'How can I live with failure?' There are no easy answers, but there are some areas for thought:

It happens to all of us

As most of us hide behind the tough-guy image, it's easy to feel that you're the only one with a failure to live with, but don't be deceived. We've all tasted failure of some sort, and we will have to taste it again. It helps to realize this—it takes away some of the isolation.

It can be a creative experience

Failure exposes our fallibility. This gives us the chance to examine our lives more honestly. It isn't easy, but most people would be honest enough to say that the hard times have done more for them as people than the soft ones. It depends on whether you're prepared to stop pretending that it hasn't happened, and are prepared to let the experience teach you. Hard to write, but like so many others, I've been through it myself, and I know this to be true.

God knows how to deal with it

God understands all about men. Despite what we are like, each of us is unique and precious to him. He doesn't promise to prevent us from exposure to failure—that would only demean us, by depriving us of the fullness of life's experience —but he knows how to make use of it so that we become better men. This is where his ways are so radically different from the ways of the world. We so easily write off failures, but God uses them. This may be hard for some to believe, but the lives of great men in the Bible show it to be true.

Failures make us more useful to God

Failures feel useless and can't see a way ahead. We feel that we have no value, no purpose, no usefulness. But God finds failures more useful and useable than successes—another radical departure from the ways of the world. He knows that men who have failed have less confidence in themselves and more in him.

Failure is very much a spiritual experience, giving opportunity to learn more about ourselves and about God. Far from being the end of the world, it can be the doorway to a richer and fuller experience of life. Are you prepared to see it this way?

What have I got to worry about?

Men don't worry! We're well-balanced and capable people, able to handle every difficulty with calm authority. This is what we would like others to believe as well. There's only one problem with this way of thinking—it's an absolute lie! Men do worry, and our worries are made worse by not sharing them.

As I write this, the following are worrying me:

* I'm worried about my children. Will they turn out all right?
* I'm worried for my wife. Will she be safe while I'm away?
* I'm worried about my job. Am I any good at it?
* I'm worried about my life. It sometimes seems so empty.
* I'm worried about money. Can I pay the bills?

What would your current list look like?

These worries are the background of my life. They're not too bad when things are going well, but when something big happens to upset me, these other worries crowd in on me, demanding attention.

We've all got things to worry about. We've all got to run our lives, handle our time, hold down a job, or face a non-work situation. We're all trying to keep our marriages right, to bring up our children, to pay our way and sort out right from wrong. We're all concerned with our lifestyle and our society. We're all getting older, facing facts about our health and our future. At any time, one or more of these areas will give us cause for worry. Some men prefer to give the impression that they're perfect, but I've reached a stage where I recognize the fact that I'm weak and fallible. This doesn't make me less of a man, although it does rule me out of the tough-guy league.

So how can we live with our worries? It will take time and courage. Here are some of the steps on the way:

Be realistic

Don't try to pretend that you don't have worries—rather face them honestly and openly. This takes great courage.

Keep a balance

Worry is only part of life. Look for the good and positive things around you as you face times of worry. This doesn't take the worries away, but it puts them in perspective. What good and positive things are in your life at the moment?

Sort them out

Sometimes many things worry me at once. When this happens I sit down and try to untangle them. This takes time, but at the end of it I feel more relaxed. At least I feel that I have done something, and isolating individual worries makes them less frightening.

Talk to a friend

We were never meant to handle our burdens alone. This is part of the legacy of the tough-guy image. It's forced us to be secretive, and to struggle on alone. Consequently many men have been broken unnecessarily. Let me encourage you with all my heart to find someone you can talk to regularly. It won't be easy because there is a strong resistance inside to sharing worries, but once you get into the habit you will find such release.

Jesus understands all about worry, and his words are an encouragement to worried men:

> So do not start worrying: 'Where will my food come from? or my drink? or my clothes?'...Your Father in heaven knows that you need all these things. Instead, be concerned above everything else with the Kingdom of God and with what he requires of you,

and he will provide you with all these other things. So do not worry about tomorrow; it will have enough worries of its own (Matthew 6:31–34).

How can I be secure?

I was walking through London with a friend of mine recently, and as it began to get dark, we found that we had come into a very dark and unsafe part of the city. There were some very strange people around, and although I'm not small, or particularly weak, I felt at some risk. I was glad to reach a more well-lit and busy area. No onlooker would have been aware of my feelings. It would have seemed to them that I hadn't a care in the world.

From the outside, men may look very secure in the way they handle life, but this is so often a front, like so much of a man's life. Inwardly many of us are very aware of the lack of security in our lives. We have to appear confident, yet we know that our jobs, our marriages and our children, our health and our future are often at risk.

It is not a sign of weakness to recognize our insecurity. Life by its very nature is insecure. We can easily be swept aside from our recognized pathways by illness, tragedy or the unexpected. Our lives are fragile things, and we do not know when our heart will stop beating, when we will meet a criminal's bullet, or our car will be involved in a fatal smash. We have to walk confidently in a world that has shown a million times over that it can destroy us in an instant.

The world tries to push our doubts out of the way. Our lives get full of material things, our marriages and families, our work and holidays. But the honest man knows that while these things are pleasant, they do not bring real security. I followed this path, like so many other men, but I could not find the security that would allow me to make the most of life's challenges and opportunities. I believed that I was as tough and able as the next man, but I knew that I was living a lie. All my bluster and arrogance only served to show me how much insecurity there was in my life. I always wanted to be popular, so that I wouldn't be alone. As I got to know God better, I was able to be honest about my need for security, and I found it in him.

The benefits:

* I've been able to live at peace with myself. I know that he will never let me down.
* I've been able to be a much more fulfilled person. I feel that I've been released from a prison.
* Other men seem much more willing to talk honestly to someone who has been honest with himself.

I haven't got it all straight yet. I still feel insecure when faced with large groups of strangers, or when in the presence of very able people. But I know that God is with me, and that I'll always be secure in him.

Why doesn't anyone understand me?

We've just had another family dispute! When David came in from school, he wanted a shower and to get his homework done. He had obviously been under pressure at school and it was showing. But Mary needed to get tea eaten, because we were going to an event at the school. She tried to explain the tea situation to David, and he tried to explain to her how it was impossible for him to eat at that moment, due to his work, his shower and so on. Tempers frayed, and finally David stormed upstairs, shouting, 'Why doesn't anyone understand me?'

We've all had moments like that—when we feel that no one understands us, or even cares much about how we feel. But before we throw this accusation at others—perhaps a wife or close friend—let's be honest: do we really understand ourselves?

A friend of mine once made this statement about me in public: 'Jim's a straightforward person.' For years I went along with this, believing it was true. But one day I decided to face reality. I didn't understand myself, so to get angry with others for not understanding me was unfair. My friend was being sympathetic, but he was totally wrong. I'm a complicated person. There's much I don't understand about myself. But now that I've faced this fact I feel more confident. Sometimes I do unpredictable things, say the wrong things, misunderstand, or lose my temper without reason. Sometimes I'm depressed for no reason, and I don't handle criticism, hostility and pressure well. This doesn't make me a case for mental treatment, but it is the truth about myself. How do *you* make out when you try to understand yourself?

Trying to understand ourselves is important, yet for many

men it's a quest they've never undertaken, because they've been convinced by the tough-guy image that men don't do this sort of thing. But if we expect others to understand us, then there's got to be some desire on our part to help them, by searching for ourselves. It is in this search that we abandon the tough guy, and become the men that God intended us to be. How can we go about it?

Recognize the inner desire

There's got to be an inner desire to make the search. It's there, because we're a race that is born to ask questions, but the tough-guy image has suppressed our questioning nature. Are you ready to start?

Find our feelings

We've got to find our feelings, to listen to them, and to let them guide and teach us. Many have lost touch with feelings altogether. Start examining how you feel about certain situations, and let this process lead you on to understand other feelings. Don't suppress hurt, but try to understand why you hurt.

Find a quiet place

If you do this it is easier to get things in perspective. It doesn't have to be far away—it could be in a park, by a stream, in the shed. It's good to be quiet and take time to think, especially in our action-packed lives.

Talk to a trusted friend

To have a trusted friend, who will listen to you as you talk and explore, is of great value. If you're married, this person should be your wife. Perhaps you need someone else as well, but she should be the primary friend.

Be patient

It takes time to understand yourself and for others to understand you.

I keep going along this path in the conviction that God understands me. No matter how complicated it gets, he knows all there is to know. So for me, it's not a quest without a guide, but it's a journey with an end.

How can I cope with pain?

Before my son Philip died, I knew very little about pain. I had experienced the odd bad moment, and as a minister I had been with people in moments of agony, but nothing had prepared me for the agony of losing our child.

I learnt so much about pain through that experience. I learnt that pain changes us. It certainly changed me out of all recognition. I learnt that pain hurts like nothing else on earth, and I learnt that pain can, given the will and the opportunity, make us stronger, more compassionate people.

I also discovered what a lie the tough-guy image is, and how totally ineffective it is in the presence of pain. Taking it 'like a man' is impossible when everything is a blur of hurt, and it doesn't open the way to explanations, understandings, or new beginnings. And with pain, we desperately need all three.

Pain can be a great spur. When it comes, men are helped to consider their values and their purpose in life. We know that we are inadequate, and we're open to the possibility of outside help. Many a man has found Jesus Christ to be a true friend through pain.

Of course some men will deny the reality of pain, and try to live normally. They throw themselves into work, or into a hobby. No one should despise men who try to face pain in this way—but it won't work. Those of us who have been through intense pain and agony know this is no way out. Pain, like acid, will eventually corrode the strongest defences.

I learnt that those in pain don't always want advice, so I suggest some ways forward here with diffidence. But there are some things that might help you through, and I share them here in the hope that I can encourage you.

You are not alone

Philip only lived for three hours, and I thought that as a well-balanced sort of person I would be able to cope. I was totally unprepared for the way in which the pain of grief would really hurt me. We're not used to it of course—there are pain killers for everything these days, and so we are insulated from pain to a certain extent. Perhaps knowing that others have also experienced the sheer reality of pain will encourage you.

Don't expect an instant cure

We live in an instant age, but pain is a long-term and lasting condition. Expecting an instant cure is unreal. Settling for a long endurance is the realistic approach.

Find support in other people

Pain cannot be endured alone for very long. I tried to keep my feelings about Philip hidden. I managed it for a year and nearly went insane with the pain. We need to be able to share it with people who will listen.

Accept that pain is a muddle

Men like rational explanations, but pain defies rationale. It's a mixture of experiences, overlapping at times, and this stirs our feelings up. Are you trying to be too rational about it?

Pain brings compassion

If you're going through pain, then you have an understanding of others in the same position. This should make you a more compassionate person—one in whom others might choose to confide about their pain. This is one of the creative sides of pain. Does it apply to you?

Pain is a spiritual experience

Christ has experienced every sort of pain—physical and emotional. He's been rejected, betrayed, isolated, humiliated, ignored and ultimately murdered. There isn't much we can tell him about pain. Perhaps he's got something to offer you.

How can I face getting old?

I'm thirty-eight and I feel old! I thought this was just me feeling a bit off, until a friend of mine, quite out of the blue, said, 'I'm thirty-eight, and I feel that my life is slipping away.' We both laughed at ourselves, but in one sense we were both right. Our lives are passing by, and the sooner we face the fact the better.

How will we cope when our physical powers diminish, our mental grip slackens, the limits of our world get smaller, and we are dependent on others for the essentials of life? How will we manage when death, which has always been a threat, becomes a distinct possibility?

Questions which concern age are harder for us men to face, because the ageing process threatens so much that we hold valuable—our physical strength, our ability to stand up for ourselves, to think rationally, to provide. So is it possible for us to face getting old? I believe that it is, if we recognize the following:

It's a fact from birth

We fall into the habit of thinking that we grow old when we retire. Retirement is a change of lifestyle, but it isn't the beginning of ageing. We begin to age from the moment we are born. Few of us can do at thirty what we could do at eighteen. Let's adopt a more realistic attitude to ageing, rather than letting an arbitrary retirement age affect us so much.

It's not all bad

As the years pass, there are some things that I can do better now than when I was eighteen or thirty. I've more experience and more opportunity. It was nice to be eighteen, but I prefer life now, and I believe that it's going to get better, even though the ageing process will continue.

There are Christian strengths to assist

For the Christian, there are many strengths in the ageing process.

* We already have a framework of eternity. We know that physical life ends, but that our spiritual destiny is safe in God's hands.
* We have a sense of worth and purpose which is outside of our own feelings and experiences. God loves us for ourselves—no matter whether we're old and grey or young and keen.
* Suffering can be taken into God's plan, so although we get hurt as much as anybody else by physical decay, we know that 'the surpassing glory belongs to God'.

As we grow old, there are many good and exciting experiences in store for us. There are many painful ones too, of course, but life is a mixture of joy and sorrow, whatever our age. We need not be negative to ageing, and the Christian man can look forward to his latter years with a special confidence.

How can I face death?

Of all the questions that I have tackled, this is one that I know will be common to all readers. We all have to face death, but how can we live so that death is not a threat or a fear?

I've come across a number of reactions to this question. Do any of them apply to you?

Don't think about it

Many people live without even considering the facts of life. Ignoring the evidence, they hope that it will never happen to them. They are like the man who reads: 'Warning! Cigarette smoking can damage your health' on the side of the packet and is so shocked he gives up reading. This attitude towards death has little to recommend it.

When you're dead, you're dead

Other people live with the conviction that since death is the total end of all life, they might as well ignore it, and do as much as they can while they are alive. They are in fact putting their faith in no faith. It sounds good when things are going well, but isn't so satisfying when death is a real possibility. It wouldn't get much of a hearing from passengers sitting on a plane that was about to crash. If the things in which we fundamentally believe can't pass a test like this, then are they really worth believing?

I'll be all right

Many others believe that if and when they die, they will have nothing to fear. They are trusting that their good lives will gain them access to heaven, always assuming there is such a place. This has always seemed to me to be the biggest folly of all. If we're really honest with ourselves, we know that there isn't much good in our lives—in fact quite the opposite. It's hard to imagine that a God who is a just judge will overlook all the filth, because we've done the odd good deed. The earthly equivalent would be pardoning a convicted criminal because he was very good to the old lady next door and occasionally collected for charity! This would never happen in an earthly court, and it certainly will never happen in the heavenly one.

Stifle your fear

Many others are afraid of death, but won't admit it. Yet there is no shame in admitting to this fear because it seems a sensible reaction to an apparently awful experience which has unknown consequences.

The Christian's answer

As a Christian I am able to face death without fear, and even with expectation. I know that for me, death is merely a gateway to a fuller and deeper relationship with Christ. There is no great unknown, no foreboding, no judgement— just his presence for ever. This conviction has nothing to do with the quality of my life, but rests on Christ's death and rising again. He has opened the way to eternal life, and because I trust him, and only because of that, I can pass through with confidence. This gives a great meaning and depth to the whole of my life—both sides of death.

Which of the ways of facing death is yours? Which do you think will bring the most satisfaction? Is it time for a change? You won't have for ever to make up your mind.

SECTION TWO

Marriage

Why should I get married anyway?

A friend of mine has just announced his engagement and the date of his wedding at the same time—even though he's not planning to get married for over a year. His family were amazed that he should have things arranged so far ahead, but as he pointed out: 'If you want to get the dates you want, and the place you want for your reception, you've got to book early!'

Despite many gloomy forecasts, marriage seems as popular as ever, and there are very good reasons for it:

We're made to share

Men and women want a way in which they can express their deep commitment to each other. Through its public ceremony and its promises, marriage makes this possible. Despite the alternative of living together, the vast majority of us still prefer the institution of marriage.

Children need security

Men and women still believe that marriage provides the most secure framework for the bringing up of children. It doesn't always work out of course, but millions of us owe much to the secure marriages which brought us to adulthood, and are trying to provide the same security for our children.

God made us to marry

Marriage is part of God's plan and purpose for his creation. He made this clear in the very beginning when he said: 'That is why a man leaves his father and mother and is united with his wife, and they become one' (Genesis 2:24).

Marriage is part of God's plan, and that's why it has survived, and why many couples have made it work, despite all the obstacles.

It's very rewarding

Marriage brings many problems, as some of the questions in this section will show, but despite these problems and in some cases because of them, it's a lot of fun, deeply satisfying and fulfilling.

What is love?

What were you doing on the 23rd August 1969? What's more, do you remember what you were saying? I remember clearly because it was my wedding day, and I was promising my wife that I would love and care for her until the day I died.

I expect you promised something similar on your wedding day, but what exactly is this 'love' that we promised so faithfully to give to this special woman? There are many questions about love that we have to face, both before and during our marriages:

* How do I know that I love this particular woman enough to want to spend my whole life with her?
* How do I know what I'm offering my wife is real love?
* How do I know that our love is still growing?

These are difficult questions for men, and made more difficult by the fact that we're not given to sharing our emotions and sometimes feel that talk about love is sloppy or unmanly. But these are the truths that we cannot avoid:

Love is an emotion

How we feel about a woman is as important as how we think about her. Love is an infatuation, so it is a real challenge to our logical male minds.

Love is a commitment

Giving ourselves to our wives in marriage means a lasting commitment, which will mean many changes in our way of life, for the rest of our life.

Love means service

Being married means wanting the very best for our wife and being prepared to go to any lengths for her. This can be a costly business.

Love is two-way traffic

In marriage, we must be giving and receiving love. How can marriage ever work if we're unable to receive, because we're trapped by our tough-guy, unfeeling image?

Love is put into action

Ultimately, our love is expressed through the way we act. Here are some areas of action based on a very famous Bible passage—1 Corinthians 13—which might have been used at your wedding. How do you rate?

Love is patient: Are you patient? Do you try to see things from your wife's point of view? How do you react when things go wrong?

Love is kind: Are you gentle towards your wife? Are you tender? Do you provide for her needs? Do you still try to give her nice surprises as you did when you were courting?

Love is not jealous: Are you jealous of anything in her life—her friends, her gifts, her freedom?

Love is not ill-mannered: Are you a considerate man? Do you respect her privacy? Are you violent towards her, either physically or emotionally?

Love is not selfish: Do you ever put your needs and wants before hers?

Love does not keep a record of wrongs: Do you forgive and forget, or do you keep a list of grievances, to use at the right moment?

Love is only happy with the truth: This can be a very costly course of action. Are you prepared to face the truth about yourself, your wife, your marriage, your family?

Love never gives up: True lovers need to be very determined in their love. Are you?

Any man who keeps this list before him, trying faithfully to be guided by it will always know the meaning and value of true love.

How do I choose the right woman?

I had been going out with Mary for about three months when we both began to talk about 'when we're married'. In fact it became so assumed, that I never really got round to asking her! I just knew that this was the person with whom I wanted to spend my life, and so far my feelings have been proved right—seventeen years and a bit on.

Other married people will tell different stories. There are as many ways of choosing the right woman as there are people doing the choosing.

It would be a brave man who would write a guide to choosing the right woman, but there are some ideas that could go into such a book:

Choosing is a two-way process

We don't go out into the market place and choose a wife. There has to be mutual attraction and mutual willingness. We might feel we have met the right woman, but if she isn't attracted to us, then that's it. She has as much right to say 'no' as we have to say 'yes'.

Courting is necessary

If we're going to discover whether there is a mutual attraction, then we have to spend time together. That's the value of the courtship process. It helps establish whether we're 'just good friends' or whether there's more to it. This process takes time, and we men are often too aggressive. We need to learn patience and gentleness. Taking time is important—a lifetime is a long time to live with a mistake.

Emotions have a say

Men are not encouraged to listen to their emotions, but finding the right wife is as much an emotional experience as it is a rational one. We've got to learn to listen to what our emotions are saying, rather than trying to suppress them.

Consider the cost

Marriage is a lifetime commitment to a woman. A lot has to be sacrificed to have marriage: our complete independence, many of our rights and privileges, and the demands of our self-centred nature. Marriage is a great joy, but there is a cost, and it's good to be aware of it before getting married.

Don't expect Miss Perfect

A number of my friends are wanting to get married, but they can't find Miss Perfect. I know why, but sadly they don't, and so they remain single. Love does not make us blind to the faults and weaknesses in others, but we can love someone despite them and make a marriage work.

Allow God to lead

An older lady of my church always used to say, 'Marriages are made in heaven.' In one sense, Christians believe her! We believe that God has a plan for our lives, and that if marriage is in his plan, then he will bring along the wife of his choice. This doesn't make the search any easier for us, nor does it spare us the embarrassments, but it does give us confidence, whether we marry or not.

Know when to say 'no'

Sometimes people get married because they haven't got the courage to say 'no', even though it's obvious that the marriage won't work out. I married a couple once who insisted on marriage, despite many indications that this wasn't a good idea. After two years of violence they split up. But another man called off his marriage only two weeks before the ceremony, because he wasn't sure he was doing the right thing. Who had the greater courage?

What happens if I didn't choose the right woman?

For a number of reasons, a man may become disillusioned with his marriage. He may discover, for example:

* She isn't the girl he thought she was.
* Marriage is proving tougher than he thought.
* Disputes and disagreements seem to be common.
* Relatives interfere.
* His social life is suffering. He can't have all his own way.

Under these circumstances it's so easy to say, 'I've married the wrong woman.' Before we do, however, there are some questions we have to face about ourselves

Are we expecting too much too soon?

We live in an instant age, but unlike coffee, marriage isn't instant. A ceremony doesn't make a marriage—many years of effort do. Have you given up trying without working hard?

Do we spend enough time with her?

Do you spend time talking with your wife about how you feel and how she feels about the marriage? If you don't share, then the marriage will never grow.

Do we have a servant heart?

Is your attitude to your wife right? The Bible teaches that she must be everything to you—that her needs and wants must be uppermost in your mind. Do you behave fairly towards her, or does she have many grounds for complaint?

Do we demonstrate our love?

Do you love her? Do you show that love through what you say, what you do and how you treat her? Our wives need demonstrations of our love towards them.

Do we need help?

Will you look for help in your marriage, or are you too arrogant or afraid to ask for it? Ministers, social workers, marriage guidance, trusted friends—there's plenty of help around, if you really want it. It depends on how much you think your marriage is worth.

Do we see her point of view?

Do you know how your wife feels about the marriage? She might feel that some of the faults are hers, but she needs the chance to share with you, knowing you will listen.

Even when these questions have been faced, some men feel that they really have made a mistake. What hope is there then?

God can change any situation

It has been said: 'Thanks be to God who raises the dead.' Your marriage may be at the point of death, but it hasn't got to die. God could revive it, although it may be a very costly process for both of you.

Determination

Many marriages have survived against all the odds, because one of the partners just won't give up. Maybe you've got to adopt the determined approach—it suits the nature of a man to do so. It's a question of how much your wife is worth to you.

Your wife could do it

Have you the humility to admit that perhaps your wife will be the one to save the marriage?

Is divorce an option?

The marriage commitment is for life. If men are not prepared for this commitment, then they don't have to get married. As a minister I have seen many marriages end with very little cause, but there are some that I have been glad to see end:

* Where there has been excessive violence towards one partner.
* Where children are getting seriously damaged, or placed at great risk.

But I firmly believe that these cases should be the exception.

How do I know I'm treating her fairly?

I collected our youngest from school recently, and when I got home Mary said, 'I'm getting behind with the washing. Will you help me?' A few years ago, I would have made some feeble excuse about being tired or busy, but I've changed a lot since then, and not only did I do the washing, but I did some of the ironing as well.

If we want to treat our wives fairly, then first of all we've got to know what kind of husbands we are meant to be. The Bible guides us in this.

Loving

We are not just to love our wives, we are to love and care for them more than we love and care for ourselves. Is this your guideline? It's an easy one to understand. All we have to do is to see how we would feel, or what we would like, and give that measure and more to our wives.

Head of the home

We are to be ultimately responsible for what goes on in our homes. This is a heavy responsibility, for to be the standard setter means that we have to be more disciplined than others, and more aware of issues and consequences. We are to carry out this responsibility as servants, there to serve our wives and to provide a framework in which they can grow and develop.

Considerate

We are to be considerate and well mannered towards our wives. We are also to be tender and gentle, to counter the hardness of the world.

Protective

Women are in no way intellectually inferior to men, but they are open to abuse, both physical and emotional, from men. As husbands, we are to provide protection against all abuse.

Sharing

Part of our headship responsibility is to share all the decisions of the marriage with our wives. We have no right to dominate, or to make arbitrary decisions.

Wanting the best

The husband who cares about his wife wants only the very best for her. He wants her to have pleasure, satisfaction, joy and peace. He wants her to be the very best woman she can possibly be, whatever the cost to him.

By these guidelines, a man can measure whether he's treating his wife fairly. How do you measure up? You might like to ask yourself:

* Do you still tell your wife you love her? When did you last do so? When did she last have a day off from the responsibility of house and family? When did you last surprise her with a present?
* When did you last act as head of your home and family? How did your wife feel? Was it a good or a bad experience for her?
* Are you considerate towards her? Does she get time to herself? Are her personal needs met? Many women make do, or squeeze essential items out of the shopping budget. Does your wife have to do this? Do you know what she needs at this moment? Are you considerate of her emotions and the pressures on her as a woman?
* Do you allow her to walk out alone late at night? Are there certain people/pressures she needs protecting from?
* Do you find time to share decisions with her? What decision did you last share?
* Do you look for chances for her to become a better person?

Am I meeting her needs?

Mary and I took our six-year-old back to school today after the summer break. At the school gate, he started to cry. I told him not to be silly. Mary cuddled him. Totally different responses, yet each of us thought we had reacted well!

Just as men and women react differently, so we have very different needs. This may be stating the obvious, yet many husbands—myself included—fail to see the obvious. We so easily assume that we are meeting needs, when in fact we are not doing so, or doing so very badly.

The best way to find out what the needs of our wives are, and whether we're meeting them, is to sit down with them regularly and talk it over. In fact this regular sharing is an essential part of marriage maintenance. Sometimes our wives are too concerned for us and they hide their real needs, so we need to be sensitive towards them, listening with our feelings, as well as with our ears. Are you sensitive in this way?

The Christian husband will be praying regularly for his wife, and not only will this make him much more aware of her needs directly, but at the same time God will be bringing needs to his mind.

Here are some areas of need that I've come to recognize in Mary. It's not meant to be a complete list, as it's a very personal observation, but it might be a useful measure for your own marriage.

* *Tenderness*. We live in a very harsh world, but I can help Mary to live in it and to achieve her potential by being tender towards her.
* *Respect*. This is so important in a close relationship where familiarity can so easily breed contempt and bad manners.

* *Time*. She needs time on her own and with me.
* *Protection*. It's a dangerous world for women, but they don't always realize it. I can provide protection against the emotional and the physical dangers.
* *Support*. A wife's job is very demanding, especially if there are children.
* *Confidence*. I can so easily undermine Mary's confidence, so I have to make every effort to build it.
* *Encouragement*. It means a lot to get this from a husband, but again familiarity can so easily lead me to forget or deny it. 'Thank you' doesn't take much effort to say, but can mean so much.
* *Consideration*. I need to try and see things from Mary's point of view.
* *Time for her own interests and friends*. If this is to happen, I have to make time to give her time.
* *Money*. She has as much right to what we have as I have.
* *Sex*. I have to try and understand her needs, as they are very different from mine. I need to be tender and gentle, not aggressive.
* *Help with decisions*. This is especially hard when I'm tired. I've no right to say, 'I've had a hard day, I need to sit down.' It's so easy for me to fail to understand how demanding the children are, all day every day.
* *Commitment*. She needs to know that I'm completely behind her in all that she does. She also needs to know that I'm not looking at or getting involved with other women. She needs to know that I am committed to her for life.

Perhaps there are some areas of need you would like to add from your own observation?

I was a very slow starter in meeting Mary's needs, and I regret it. But once I realized my mistake, I started to correct it. I've much to learn, but I am getting there. If you feel that you haven't been getting it right, it's never too late to start. Our wives are very loyal to us and will respond to our care and concern.

Is she meeting my needs?

Yesterday I worked on my word processor all day. By the evening I was tired, but I had to keep going to finish an article. Mary looked round the door and said, 'Don't you think you've done enough for today?' She was right, of course, but I was annoyed. How dare she come and tell me what to do and how to run my day?

But then I began to see it another way. Perhaps she was trying to help me, rather than annoy me? After a few more minutes I realized that she was right and switched off the machine.

It's hard sometimes to realize that our wives do know our needs, and can help us with them. Of course they can't help us if we don't tell them. These questions have to be faced:

* Do you take time to share your needs with your wife? If you don't, then you can't turn round and accuse her of not meeting them. Some she can guess at, but not all.
* Are you prepared to admit that you have needs? It's so easy to hide behind the tough-guy image and pretend that you're able to manage.
* Are you honestly prepared to let her help you? There's no point in sharing if you've no intention of listening, or of receiving the help offered.

What are the needs that we want to have met? Here's my list, and it's very personal to me, but it might give you something to measure against.

* *Acceptance.* I need to know that my wife will accept me as I am—with all my faults and weaknesses.

* *Security*. I need to know that I am secure in her love, whatever I may say or do, or whatever may happen.
* *Position*. I need to know that I am the head of my home, and that my wife will allow me this position.
* *Value*. I need to know that I make a real contribution to her life.
* *Forgiveness*. I need to know that Mary will forgive me for my mistakes, which can be numerous.
* *Tolerance*. I need to know that Mary will put up with my moods, which are many and various, and will allow me the room to have them.
* *Fun*. I like life, and I need a chance to express my joy, and share it with my wife. I also need her to help me see the funny side of life when I'm getting depressed.
* *Physical*. I need to be touched and to touch my wife. I want her to enjoy intimacy and intercourse.
* *Peace*. I need to know that I can relax and do nothing sometimes.
* *Release*. I need a chance to release my tensions and anxieties.
* *Sharing*. I need someone who will share my lonely job and my lonely world.

The Christian man approaches needs from a different perspective. He wants the best for his wife, and so he gives himself to her needs. As he does this, he finds that many of his own needs are met. He also knows that God understands all his needs, and this gives him the confidence to share those needs with his wife.

When the sharing process breaks down from either side, the marriage deteriorates. The only way forward then is through forgiveness and starting again.

Can I tell her what I'm feeling?

I don't find it easy to tell Mary how I'm feeling, even though she is a very understanding person. When I'm low or worried, it takes me a long time to talk about it with her. It was nearly two years before I could start telling her how hurt I was at the death of our baby son. I bottled the feelings up, and just couldn't get them out.

Why do so many of us find it hard to share our feelings? There are a number of reasons:

* The tough-guy image has captured us, and we feel that showing our feelings is weakness.
* We've lost the art of sharing our feelings. Now we don't even know where to begin, even if the time seems right.
* We've tried it once, got hurt, and so made a promise to ourselves that we would never get hurt again—so we lock our feelings away.
* We feel that no one would understand us, even if we did share.
* We think that other people wouldn't be interested in us, and that we would be wasting their time.

Against this kind of background, it is always going to be hard to work out a sharing relationship with our wives. Having accepted this fact how can we go about it?

Be brave

In the end, we've got to take our courage in both hands, and begin to tell our wives about ourselves and our inner feelings. It's always going to be risky, but it's a chance we've got to take if a real sharing relationship is going to develop.

Trust her

We've got to believe that our wives will understand, or at least make the effort to understand, and that they won't try to hurt us with the things we are sharing with them. Part of our trust means that we're committed to going on sharing, even if there are times when it seems to be going wrong.

Take it easy

Mary and I found that when we started being honest with each other it was better to share little and often, rather than all at once. Too much at once would easily overwhelm her, whereas the 'little and often' approach brought a gradual build up of trust, which opened the way for deeper trust and deeper sharing.

Know that sharing is two way

The more I was open with Mary, the more she was able to be open with me. This two-way process helped us both, and our trust in each other increased.

Choose the right time and place

There are right moments for sharing and there are wrong ones. Try to find the right time and place. For us it's often our local curry house. There, at the corner table, we've ironed out many an issue. Where's your place? Choosing the wrong time could be a disaster, leading to you getting hurt and setting the sharing process back many weeks or even months.

Realize that it won't be easy

It's good to accept this from the start—it makes the hurts easier to bear. Honest sharing is never easy, because it often means reliving past worries and troubles.

Remember prayer helps

Mary and I try to surround our sharing with prayer, and we find that this helps us a lot. It makes it easier to be open with each other, and helps when we both feel that we can't go any further.

You can tell her how you feel. It will be a costly process, but the price of holding all your feelings in is, in the long run, far higher.

What happens when she hurts me?

Mary often hurts me, and I'm ashamed to say I often hurt her. At our summer camp this year, I made a remark which offended her. She didn't say anything, but went off for a walk. When she didn't return I became concerned, and eventually went to find her. Later that evening, when we had both calmed down, she admitted that she had intended to hurt me by staying out as late as possible and causing me worry. We were able to talk things over and put the matter right, but it did hurt at the time. If we are going to abandon the tough-guy image, and have an open sharing relationship with our wives, we are going to get hurt and have to admit it.

In one respect the tough guy is a safer person. He has so many barriers around him that it's impossible for his wife to hurt him—or at least that's how he wants it to appear. But this is small consolation when placed against the truth: the tough-guy image is a lie which has ruined so many men and so many marriages.

Facing the fact that in a real sharing relationship our wives have the power to hurt us is a big thing. Once we understand it, we can begin to learn to control our normally retaliatory and aggressive reactions.

Here is the alternative that I'm developing. It works for me and it might give you some ideas for dealing with hurt. I am greatly helped by my knowledge of Christ, who seemed to be able to absorb pain without resorting to anger.

Recognize it

I accept now that Mary can hurt me, and when she does I don't try to shrug it off. This helps me control my reactions.

Absorb it

I used to react badly when Mary hurt me, and I still do at times, but this only resulted in two hurt people. So now I try to absorb the hurt, recognizing it for what it is, and also accepting that because I really do love Mary, I can take it. It's harder to do this, but it is a mark of genuine love. I find Christ's example the greatest help here. He didn't retaliate because he really loved, and I try to do the same. It is not easy.

Forgive

It's no good absorbing pain if we only allow it to cause resentment. We have to learn to forgive the other person. When we handle hurt like this, it's amazing how we are able to see things from the other person's point of view. Perhaps Mary is only hurting me because she's hurt, or tired, or frustrated. It's always possible that at the root of it, something I have done is responsible for her hurting me.

Talk it out

Hurts can be shared after they have passed. This way they are turned to creative good, because they become an opportunity to share and to grow. If we can't share it with our wife because it's too difficult, then we need to talk to a trusted friend first. But this should only be the beginning of a process which leads to us sharing with our wife.

There is no easy answer to this question because dealing with hurt is always a tough assignment. But when our wife hurts us, we are faced with a very straight question: do we really love her enough to take this and any other hurt? Will we really endure anything for her?

How can we keep talking to each other?

One time, quite out of the blue, Mary decided that she wanted to tell me a lot of things that were on her mind. Unfortunately, I had a lot of things on *my* mind at the time and, to be quite honest, I didn't really listen that carefully. Laying in the bath the next day, I began to think about this, and I realized what a mistake I had made. Nothing could ever be more important than a man and wife sharing the things that matter. When I was dressed, I went to Mary and managed to persuade her to say it all again—and this time I listened. I was very fortunate that she was willing to go through a repeat performance. The opportunity might never have come again to talk over those particular matters.

Talking together about each other, and the marriage, is such a vital part of the marriage experience. It's as important as sex, but men don't always see this. There are some real enemies to talking together:

Being too busy

Life can be so busy, that there just doesn't seem to be time to talk.

Being too tired

We're so stretched, that when quiet periods come we just fall asleep.

Being too crowded

Life is full of people, all the time. In our home, our youngest gets up at 6 am, and our eldest goes to his room at 10 pm, and doesn't settle before 11 pm. There just never seems to be time to be alone.

Being too lazy

There comes a stage where we just can't be bothered to talk together.

Being too familiar

Familiarity is an enemy of marriage. We think that we know each other so well that there isn't the need to talk and share.

Being too confident

We fall into the trap of thinking that everything in the garden is rosy, so there's no need to talk.

Have you fallen into any of these traps? Mary and I have experienced most of them at different times. How can we avoid these problems and keep talking to each other?

Make the time

We always make time for things that we consider to be important. We must start seeing that talking is the most important thing in marriage.

Somewhere in a busy day, there are a few moments for you and your wife to talk. Have you found them? Every now and again, more than a few minutes is needed, and that's when we need to go out—for a walk, a meal, a drive.

Make the effort

Having time is only half of the answer. When it's been found, it has to be used. There needs to be a willingness to talk, to share and to grow together. Do you have this?

See the other point of view

Part of the talking process is seeing things from your wife's point of view. Do you make this effort?

Start again

Mary and I go through phases where we can talk openly and easily, then something happens and we hardly talk at all. It is important that these periods are brought quickly to an end, or they could lead to serious marital damage. When this breakdown of communication occurs I have a determination that we shall start talking again, no matter what the cost—apology, flowers, trip out, or whatever. I don't care if I seem to be climbing down, I want to keep talking. In the end, it's this kind of determination that finds a way through. Have you got it?

Should we have children?

Mary and I have had five children, all boys. After the birth of the youngest, I was visiting Mary in hospital and one of the staff said to me, 'Have you come to see your grandchild?' I'm seldom at a loss for words, but on this particular occasion I didn't know quite what to say. It did cause me to think, however, that perhaps the moment had come to call a halt to having more children!

There is a deep urge within our hearts to have children. This is a part of God's plan for his creation, and marriage is God's institution for ensuring not only that children are conceived, but that they have secure surroundings in which to grow and mature.

I must be honest and say that Mary and I never planned any of our children—they just arrived—but the following are some factors we consider important about having children.

They must be a joint decision

This is an intimate matter, and doesn't necessarily have to be put into too many words, but the desire needs to be in the heart of both husband and wife. In these terms, the family that Mary and I had were a joint decision. We both desired children very much. Perhaps that's part of the reason why they came.

Born in love

Mary and I have had children because we love each other, and this has been one expression of our love. Children need to be conceived in this kind of love, not out of a desire to save a marriage, or because it seems a good thing to do.

Continuing security

Children bring great joy, but also many commitments. They need a secure home, endless love and a lifetime of dedication. Children are never 'off your hands', even though they leave home and get married. As we conceive them, so we must be willing to make this kind of lifelong commitment to them.

Conception is a risk

None of us know what birth will bring. Our baby could be perfect, or he could be handicapped. We must be committed to the child, whatever happens, and this is a very open-ended commitment.

We're in it together

Gone are the days when a husband could leave pregnancy and birth to his wife. From the moment Paul was conceived, I was with Mary all the way through and was present when he was born. I soon learnt how to feed and water him, to change his nappies and to help him get to sleep. These days, husband and wife are in it together, which is a great privilege.

A changed way of life

Life is never the same with children around. We cannot carry on with the same habits and patterns, because it's just not possible. This may appear to be a sacrifice, but children give so much in return that it doesn't seem to matter.

Whether you should have children in your marriage is very much a personal matter. You will have to give up a lot to have them, and maybe many things that you hold dear will get swept away. But as I write this, my six-year-old, whose birth I witnessed, is standing at my elbow waiting for me to go over to the park with him, and I know that for me nothing else could ever be so rewarding as children.

How can I help her to enjoy sex more?

Mary and I have been married for seventeen years, and I'm happy to say that we enjoy sex now more than ever. And I know that there is more to learn and enjoy in the years ahead.

Having said this, we have found that sex has caused much misunderstanding and confusion in our marriage. We had different expectations, and it's still something that we can get wrong. I have had to learn some lessons in this very sensitive area. They haven't been easy, but they have helped us both to enjoy sex more.

Love

The key to a fruitful sexual relationship is love. If we genuinely love our wives, for their personalities, their gifts and skills and the joy they bring to us, and if we are in the habit of telling and showing our love for them, then sexual relationships fall into their right place, as an expression of this love.

Tenderness

Our love has to be coupled with tenderness. There is enough hardness and aggression in the world already without it needing to enter our intimacy. This is important for us men to recognize, as we are aroused very quickly and our sexual urge is a very physical experience. Sometimes we can be almost raping our wives under the disguise of 'fulfilment'. This may bring some temporary satisfaction, but it will not bring genuine love, or growth in mutual understanding and fulfilment.

Wholesomeness

Health food is very popular these days, and we should carry the same desire for healthy living into our sexual relationships. Magazines, and even the local free papers, advertise what are known as 'love aids'. The suggestion is that these things will enhance our sexual experience. As husbands, it's essential that we guard against these intrusions into intimacy. They don't 'aid' love, they only demean it. The only aid a man needs in his marriage is genuine and gentle love. This will open every delightful door of intimacy.

Seeing her viewpoint

Men and women see sex in very different ways. This was something which took me a long time to realize. But as I began to learn how Mary saw and experienced things, I was able to enter more into intimacy with her. There are many books available on the subject, but why not talk to your wife over a period of time. It's well worth doing, and will make sex much more interesting and special for both of you.

Timing

I can easily finish a job on the car, wash my hands and be ready for bed! But Mary isn't like this. If she has had a bad day with the kids, she can't leave it all outside the bedroom door. She brings it with her, and it will affect our intimacy. Learning to understand and accept this is the mark of a loving husband. Sometimes we need to be content with a kiss, when we would like much more, just because of the pressures of the day on our wives. The sacrifice is worth it because women respond to this sensitive understanding.

The Christian man is willing to bring God into all of his life, and this includes sex. Mary and I are learning to pray for our intimacy, and through it as well. We sometimes feel a bit embarrassed, but we assume that God has seen it all before!

How do I divide my time between marriage and other things?

I'm in trouble again! Mary is trying to clean the house up because we've got friends coming. I helped her a bit, but while she was upstairs I crept back to my computer, and now she's discovered my crime and I'm condemned to the sink!

While we all need time with our wives, and time for our marriage and family, we also need time for other things. Personally, I need time for: work, rest and leisure, house maintenance, my friends, other family members, parents, church and being alone.

Mary has similar needs, and somehow we have got to work out a balance between time for our marriage and time for the other things. We could abandon the other things, but then our marriage would suffer, because we would become very closed in as people. Or we could just do the other things and abandon our marriage. It's a difficult balance. How can married people work it out?

Reassessing the balance

Seventeen years of trying to work this balance out has taught me that it's not an easy thing to achieve. What's more, the balance has to keep being adjusted. As the children grow up, as interests and friends change, so does the balance.

Love and understanding

Both partners need to exercise love and care, as this balance is constantly checked. Mary is very understanding towards me, and I hope that I've become more understanding towards her in recent years. Overall I suspect that women come off worse, because they are so loyal to us and so willing to let us have our own way.

Being honest

When you start doing excessive overtime, spending a lot of time on a hobby or project, or being with your friends, ask yourself these questions:

* Am I comfortable in what I am doing? Our feelings will soon start to tell us if we are being unfair towards our wives.
* Am I running away from my responsibilities? When men spend excessive amounts of time away from their wives, even with the best of reasons, it's sometimes because they won't take their responsibilities seriously.
* Is my wife getting equal time on her own? If we are going to spend time away from the marriage, then our wives have equal rights to spend time away. Is she getting time with her friends, time for rest, time for leisure? If you were to measure the time you spend alone against hers, how does she score?

How can I improve our marriage?

I'm always looking for opportunities to improve the quality of my relationship with Mary. I want to treat her better, to get closer to her, to share in the bringing up of the children, to have more fun together, to overcome the problems. I firmly believe that despite seventeen thrilling years, the best is yet to come.

I've had to face a number of issues as we've tried to improve our life together. Are any of them familiar to you?

Prepare for changes

Many times in my life, I've asked God to change circumstances. On a number of occasions, his reply has been, 'No, but I can change you.' If we want to improve our marriages, then some of the biggest changes are going to take place in us. Take an honest look at yourself—what you do, how you behave, what you say and think. If you were to make some changes in these areas, would your marriage improve?

It's not going to be easy. Even recognizing that we need to change is quite a battle for us, and then making the changes can be even harder. For me, God makes it easier. He does the changing inside, as soon as I'm willing to let him act. Then the inner changes slowly work themselves out in my behaviour and lifestyle.

Learn to listen

About four years ago, I had a real desire to make changes in myself so that Mary and I would have a better marriage. I soon discovered that Mary was perplexed at what was happening, even though she could see a great improvement. So I had to learn to listen to her, as she expressed her concerns, and to spend time explaining what was happening. Men by nature like to get on with a task. I had to learn to slow down and to listen. Do you listen to your wife?

Hope for the best

Things don't always work out in marriage. When things go wrong, it's so easy to give up, or to blame our wives. At times like this, we've got to hope and believe that things can work out, and also give our wives some credit for believing the same, instead of blaming them. Are you determined that things will improve? Do you assume the best of motives in your wife?

Don't lust

Most men look at other women who are not their wives. Learn to look and enjoy the pleasure of other women, but not to lust after them. We have to stand firm against the temptation to think lustfully. If we resist these pressures, then our relationship with our own wife will improve.

Check the balance

Are you giving enough time to your marriage? Are you giving enough time to other things—hobbies, friends, work, leisure? Have you got the balance right?

Think about it

Marriages don't just happen. They need time spent on them, and some of that time needs to be spent in thought and reflection. Where is your marriage going? How are you both feeling? Are the finances under control? Are the children happy? Time spent like this can seem a waste, but it is in fact well spent if the result is a better and more secure marriage.

Know God has a place

God really cares about our marriages and he has a plan that will result in us getting the very best from them. Time spent in his presence—both together and separately—considering the marriage will result in the very best improvements. Does God have a place in your marriage?

What will happen if I lose my job?

A man can lose his job through redundancy, industrial injury, early retirement or dismissal. Whatever the way, he will pass through a number of experiences, which will affect his marriage.

Too much time

A man without a job has too much time on his hands. His work helped to timetable his life. Now there is no set routine. This makes most men irritable and hard to live with, so it is bound to affect the marriage. He may also find that he hasn't got a place in his wife's timetable. She has worked her day out without reference to him, as he has always been away at work. Now her timetable has to be adjusted to include him, and this change isn't always smooth. Unemployment can be a very rocky time for a marriage, and underlying tensions can quickly surface.

Too little money

Losing a job usually means having to get by on less money. Most people live up to their incomes, and while many are used to pay rises, few are used to pay cuts. Long-term financial commitments, such as the mortgage, or paying for the car, now become a real problem. There is also the pressure of having to do with less, while others seem to have so much. This can cause problems both for husband and wife at home, and for children at school.

No purpose

Men function best when there's clear direction in their lives. When paid work goes, any sense of direction or purpose often goes with it. This will inevitably throw great pressure on the marriage.

But along with the problems come great possibilities—if we have the courage and the will to see them. Many marriages have been greatly enriched and strengthened through losing a job. Here are two positive factors:

More time together

Too much time creates problems, but it also makes opportunities which weren't there before—time to see the children off to school, time to shop, to visit friends, to be together. Tasks can be shared and love and confidence built up.

Chance to change

Unemployment brings a change of lifestyle and expectation. But many of us live unhealthy lifestyles and have expectations that are far from good. Losing a job gives a man a chance for an honest appraisal of himself and his marriage. This can lead to changes in marriage, thought, diet, expectation and finance. A man seldom gets a chance to do this when he's working.

Losing a job is a hard experience, and the process of adjustment is a painful one. The man who believes in God has to face exactly the same pressures as anyone else, but he does have a positive conviction that God is in charge of his life, can make some sense of what is happening and will use the experience to make him a more fulfilled and better person.

Where can I get help?

Originally I intended just to give a list of agencies that can help marriages, with their addresses. But seventeen years as a minister have taught me that it's impossible to help those who won't accept help. I've have the sorrow of watching a number of marriages die, just because people involved would not look for help and advice. It's impossible to help those who don't want help, and no list of agencies, however extensive, would be of any use to such people. But why should we not want help in our marriage, when we know that things are not right? There are a number of reasons:

Pride

Men are too proud to ask for help. We've been brought up to believe that we can handle everything on our own. This makes is particularly difficult to accept the fact that we cannot cope.

Fear

We are afraid to let others see our weakness, and we've been led to believe that difficulty in marriage is weakness.

We think we're alone

People often don't share their marital problems, so when we encounter a problem ourselves whether it's large or small, we feel that we're the only one going through it. This adds to our isolation, our desperation and depression. I've heard the basic marriage problems hundreds of times, and each time the couple involved think that they're the only ones in trouble.

We feel hopeless

We think we're beyond help. Sadly, some marriages are beyond rescue, but some problems can be resolved, or could have been resolved if they had been attended to early enough. Mostly we just need a sympathetic ear, a little understanding and time.

All marriages go though times of difficulty. Whether we survive these times or not depends on how much we value our marriage and how much we love our wives. If we really care, then there is help available. We need to choose the source of our help with care, of course, but here are some that are worth considering:

Our wife

As I've said many times, our wife should be our closest friend and ally. Maybe the problems can be overcome with some patience and time to talk and think.

Trusted friend

We may need to talk to someone who is outside the situation. Have you a trusted friend, whose judgement you have confidence in, and who will keep your confidence, but also be very honest with you?

Minister

Some people find help from talking to their minister. If you can trust him, then he will certainly keep your confidence, and may have some real insight. He has the advantage of having dealt with many marriages, and so will help you see your difficulties in perspective.

Doctor

Some doctors can be very helpful, but they are often busy in their surgeries. Try to fix a time to see them at the end of surgery so as to avoid a great queue. He might put you in touch with marriage guidance services, as might your minister.

Why are we both hurting?

Mary and I were having a heated discussion which was getting more heated by the minute. We were both being nasty to each other, until finally she shouted, 'I hate you.' This reduced us both to silence. I was stunned by her words, and she was shocked by what she had said.

I expect that this, or something similar, is a common scene in most marriages. Man and wife are very vulnerable to each other, and when tensions increase, so does the potential for hurt. The real question we face, as husbands, is how do we handle the hurt, both ours and that of our wife, so that it doesn't destroy the marriage, or lead to a long period of poor relationships?

Understand what's happening

I am slowly learning that to lash out in anger at Mary, because I have been hurt by her, is a very damaging response and only makes matters worse. I'm trying to learn the art of responding in love when things are going wrong. This is a two-way process, of course, and Mary is trying to learn to do the same when I hurt her. It breaks the cycle of anger and hurt, even though in the short term I can end up getting more hurt. Those who respond in love to hurtful things have to absorb some of the pain in order to overcome it. But I am taking this course because I really do love my wife and want the best for her.

Recognize when you are at fault

I like to think that sometimes I'm the innocent party, and that it's all Mary's fault. But the truth is that I've always played some part in what is happening, if I'm really honest with myself. Recognizing this truth makes it easier to cope with the hurt, and to finding a way to forgiveness and healing.

Forgive and start again

When we hurt each other in our marriages, the only way out is through forgiveness. It's our responsibility as husbands to be ready to forgive, without resentment. It's up to us to make the first move, even if we think that we're in the right. Many of us find this a difficult thing to do, because we are so proud. But if we truly love our wives, and want the best for them, then we'll make the first move with joy, won't we? We are faced yet again with the question which is behind many of the other questions in this section: do we truly love our wives?

Understand that love is tough

Sometimes forgiveness is not enough. If we want true reconciliation, then we have to be prepared to face the reasons for the hurt and pain. This can be a very painful process for both partners, as hard truths can often hurt. Yet if we don't get at the reasons for the hurt, they will only go on hurting again and again.

Treat hurts with love

Love is the medicine that can heal much of the damage that we do to each other. No matter how bad things have become, there is still a way back, with real tender loving care. Can your wife guarantee this from you?

As a Christian man, I struggle with hurts and forgiveness like any other husband. But I find help and strength in Christ, who seemed to know how to forgive, without losing any of his masculinity.

What can I do with my sexual urges?

I was travelling on the bus recently, and a succession of very pretty girls got on and off. It wasn't long before I was having problems with my sexual urges! Most men have to keep a firm control on their sexual desires. We are very physical, and women quickly excite us. Many women are unaware of the effect they have on us, and certain styles of dress do not help us. Single men are apt to assume that marriage puts an end to the problem, but it's an area of concern for all men— married or single.

So what can we do with our urges, so that they remain healthy?

One option open to us is to look at all women and let our urges have their way. This demeans women, treating them not as people with rights, but as objects of our sexual lusts. It also ultimately demeans us as men.

Sexual urges are not evil

We may have a problem with sex, but that doesn't make our sexual feelings wrong. We were given them by God so that the human race could be guaranteed survival. Far from being evil, they make us whole people and give us the chance to share with God in the joy of creation. When directed rightly, they give us deep personal satisfaction and a sense of fulfilment.

Men are very basic!

Men are very basic in their approach to sex. Jesus, knowing our hearts, put the challenge quite bluntly and in terms that every man will recognize as genuine: 'You have heard that it was said, "Do not commit adultery." But now I tell you anyone who looks at a woman and wants to possess her is guilty of committing adultery with her in his heart.' (Matthew 5:27–28).

I have found this helpful because at least I know what I am up against now.

Discipline

We've got to learn to control our eyes and our thoughts, and this takes a lot of effort, especially as it's often going against the habits of a lifetime. But for example:

We don't have to look. Women have lovely faces—perhaps we've got to learn to enjoy this part of them and not look elsewhere.

We don't have to think. There's no reason why our thoughts should get out of hand. Learn to cut them off, or think of something else.

We don't have to watch. Television has much on it that is unhelpful to us, but we don't have to watch it. Are you discriminating in what you watch?

We don't have to read. Newspapers and books also contain much that stimulates us in the wrong way—but we don't have to read them.

Let go

Sexual urges can still build up inside us, however much we try to discipline ourselves and we've all got to find ways of releasing them. How do you release yours? The ideal way is to turn them into creative love with your wife. There are other ways as well: getting involved in your work, breaking the chain of thinking by doing something else, such as sport, hobbies, even taking a run or a shower.

Maybe you feel that you've already lost the battle—that your urges are so out of control there's no way you can get them back under control. Perhaps you can't, but God can, if you have the courage and willingness to ask for his help.

What is unfaithfulness?

One man fell in love with a woman, even though he was married. He moved in with her, slept with her, and then divorced his wife.

One man desired another woman, even though he was married. So he carried on a clandestine relationship with her, while remaining married.

One man found that he preferred to confide in a woman he knew at work, rather than his wife. He had a deep relationship with this woman, although he didn't have a sexual relationship with her.

One man, happily married, found other women very attractive, and couldn't contain his errotic emotions towards these other women—in fact he didn't want to control them.

All these men were being unfaithful to their wives, to a greater or lesser degree. We don't always want to face this truth. We prefer to define unfaithfulness as the act of sleeping with one woman while being married to another, and so many of us feel that we are excluded. But faithfulness has much more to it than just the sexual side, and it is in this wider context that many more of us are implicated.

Unfaithfulness brings a grim harvest of doubt, mistrust and hurt. Relationships are damaged and the seeds of bitterness are sown. The real tragedy is that any man who is being unfaithful to his wife, in any way, thinks that he is escaping his problems. Unfortunately, he is probably only exchanging one set of problems for another. However green the grass looks on the other side of the fence, it still needs mowing!

How can we as husbands be more faithful, and so avoid the snares of unfaithfulness?

Love with a whole heart

Again we come back to the much asked question: Do you really love your wife with your whole heart? True love is our great defence against unfaithfulness in all its forms. Do you talk about your problems with her, love her, treat her with respect, want the very best for her, whatever the cost to yourself? Do you need to make a fresh start with her, confess some failures, break some relationships that are leading to unfaithfulness?

Be on guard

Being made the way we are, we men need to keep a very strong hold on our sexual urges. They can so easily lead us astray, and once this happens, we just get deeper and deeper into trouble.

Some men find that their wives are being unfaithful to them. It's so easy to blame the woman in these cases, but often an unfaithful wife is a woman who has not received the love and care that she needs from her husband—from you.

It is always possible to start again, if you are prepared to ask for forgiveness for your failures, and to freely forgive your wife, if she has been unfaithful. But this must be linked with a willingness to be different in the future. It's no good starting again and then repeating the same faults. This course has never been easy, but it could save your marriage. The alternative is to live a lie and watch your marriage die.

Those of us with God at the centre of our marriages still have to struggle against unfaithfulness. But from him we do receive an inner strength which helps us through the struggles to a deeper faithfulness to our wives.

Are there ever grounds for divorce?

This has never been an easy question to answer. In many countries, the State allows divorce on certain defined grounds, and so it has become relatively easy to end a marriage. In the religious field, some churches accept divorce, while others are opposed to it on biblical grounds. All churches do agree, however, that divorce should be regarded as the very last resort, and that counselling, prayer and discussion should be offered to any marriages experiencing difficulty.

Many couples are not prepared to accept this kind of help. If it isn't working out they resort to the divorce courts. Perhaps they've become infected with the twentieth-century desire to have everything 'instant', and expect their marriages to be instantly successful. Perhaps they believe that a ceremony makes a marriage, without realizing the years of effort and love that have to be spent to make a marriage secure and successful.

As a committed Christian, I believe that God's intention is that marriage should be for life. I'm far from Mr Perfect, but I've always taken my marriage promises seriously. When I made them, I made them towards Mary for life, and with God's help I'm going to keep them. Millions like me have the same determination, and somehow we've got to pass this on to millions of others. But, as a minister, I have had to deal with many breaking and broken marriages, and I have come to accept that some—and many less than actually happen— are beyond redemption. I know that nothing is beyond God's redeeming love, and so I suppose I must appear a little confused and inconsistent. But I've had to deal with the reality of the situation. These are the circumstances that have made me glad to see a marriage end:

* Where there is violent abuse of the woman.
* Where there is violent abuse or sexual harassment of the children.
* Where both partners are damaging each other so badly that they need to live apart.
* Where the marriage has been dead for years, and all that's needed is the funeral.

I can only repeat that these are the exceptions rather than the rule, and that despite everything God can redeem the unredeemable.

What will happen if she dies?

Over the years, I have had to help many people face the loss of their partner, and one thing has become very clear—a man who loses his wife is in for a harder time than a woman who loses her husband. We have so much against us:

* Most of us are not used to shopping, cooking or doing housework. We can learn, but it's not an easy time of life in which to learn it.
* We can find it much harder to make friends, and so we're more prone to loneliness. Most of the friends we had we probably shared with our wife, which makes us feel even more alone.
* We are much less likely to cry or show our feelings. This is a big handicap when coming to terms with bereavement.
* We are not equipped to bring up children on our own, especially if they are young.

There's no way round the toughness of it all, but there are some positive things, even in the middle of great sorrow. I can only write this because I went through it with the loss of our son.

Grief can be survived

Millions have found their way through grief. We have emerged very different men and we have memories that hurt, but we have survived.

Becoming a better man

Grief can make us better men or bitter men. We can finish up angry and bitter, or we can become more sensitive, more caring and more aware of the needs of others. The choice is yours, but there is a choice. Bitterness and anger are not inevitable.

Facing memories

There's no survival without coming to terms with the pain, the sorrow and the memories. These have to be faced, and men find this difficult, because it means letting their emotions have a say in their lives.

Recognizing our need of others

Grief cannot be survived completely alone—anyone trying it will finish up in a very sorry state. We need other people to share our grief with, and we need the courage to share what's happening to us. However independent we may feel we've just got to accept that we cannot go it alone.

Discovering God

God has everything to offer a grieving man. He understands and cares, because he has suffered himself. He doesn't need to be told what's happening to us. Many a man has found the reality of God through grief.

SECTION THREE

Family

Are we a family?

A few years ago, breakfast in our house was a very 'unfamily' affair. People would arrive when they felt like it, take what they wanted and then leave. It was unlikely that anyone would even bother to say 'good morning'.

Then I began to see that as a family we were missing out on a very important family experience—starting the day together. We sat down as a family, talked this over and as a result, the breakfast experience underwent a radical change. We agreed on a fixed time and we all arrived at that time. The children wanted a cooked breakfast and I agreed to cook it. No one was ever late, because if they were late, they found that someone else had eaten their food! Slowly a real family feeling came into breakfast. It became a short but important time together, and it was a sign of better things to come.

We began to learn what it meant to be a family, and this affected every part of our lives—both the time we spent together and the time we spent apart. We began to support and encourage each other. If anyone was successful, we all rejoiced, and if anyone was down-hearted, we all tried to provide comfort and cheer.

This change, which came about after many years of marriage, started because I realized that I had to change my attitude and behaviour towards others. The husband and father sets the standard for so much in his home, and I came to realize that I wasn't setting much of a family standard in mine. It hasn't been easy and we've still a lot to learn.

These are the essentials that I had to grasp in order for us to become a family. Do you need to consider them as well?

The father loves his wife

Family life flows from this simple and obvious truth. As husband and wife share their love together and show it to the children, so the family will grow in commitment. Do you really love your wife, sharing your whole life with her? Are you concerned with her well-being above all else?

The father is totally committed to the family

The family needs the security of knowing that it is built on a rock of total commitment. For me this means that I am committed to Mary until the day I die, and Mary has exactly the same commitment to me and to the children. Within this security, the family can survive its problems and disputes, and have great fun. Without it, there is always an element of uncertainty.

The father loves his children and only wants the best for them

I'm not afraid to discipline my children, or say hard things to them. But I'm always wanting the very best for them, and I want to encourage them in any way I can. Do your children know that this is true about you?

The father is open to God

It's hard to be a good father without a reference point, and I find mine in God, my heavenly Father. He guides me, as I guide the family. It's my great privilege to be his kind of father, and through my behaviour I hope and pray that my family will get a glimpse of what he is like.

What's my job in the family?

There may have been a time when this question did not need to be asked. The husband would have earned the money and the wife would have kept house. But with a high level of unemployment, and the rising tide of feminism, men have become uncertain of their position and job in the family. The confusion is increased because we live in a society that has abandoned the Bible as its basic guideline, for what God says about a man's role is clear:

The father is head of the home

We are not, however, to dominate the family. We need to see ourselves as servants of the family, keeping a careful check on our behaviour and lifestyle. We must discipline ourselves, and see that the needs of the family are foremost in our minds.

The father is to support his wife

Husbands often treat their wives badly, whereas they have every right to expect nothing but support and encouragement from us. It's our responsibility to see that they get it. This way, they will become the women God intended they should be, and the family will enjoy the benefit.

The father is to encourage the children

Our society is a competitive one and there is much criticism. The father counters this by encouraging his children. This means being interested in their world, spending time trying to understand both them and it, and being willing to see things from their point of view.

The father is to have time for the family

Families don't just happen—they need time spent on them. We need to ensure that each family member is getting some of our time, and that the family as a whole is spending some time together. Spending time with our family is worth a thousand presents to them. We are giving them the best present of all—ourselves.

The father disciplines

The family cannot flourish if there is no discipline, and this is our responsibility. It's a heavy one, and it must be based on a genuine love for each member. It also carries with it the responsibility to be disciplined ourselves. If we are undisciplined, we will have no credibility in the eyes of our family, and our discipline will fail.

We are at the very heart of the family, setting the tone and standards for the others to measure up against and to follow. It's a big responsibility. How do you measure up? Here are some questions that I have asked myself about myself and my family:

* Do I discipline my own life? What needs checking at this moment?
* Do I support my wife, and does she know it? Have I been guilty of lowering her esteem in the presence of the family?
* When did I last encourage each member of my family? What was the occasion? When did I last discourage my family? What was the occasion? What do I intend to do about it?
* When did I last give one hour of my time to each member of my family?
* When did I last get the family together, so that we could do something together?
* When was I last called on to discipline a family member? Was I fair?
* When did I last make a decision, or help with one concerning the family?
* When did I last help the family understand something about God?

Do I want my children to grow up like me?

The other night I was woken by the sound of one of my younger children coughing. I was sure it was Paul because I've heard him so many times, so I went straight to his room. But he was fast asleep. I discovered that it was our two-year-old, Stephen, who now coughs just like Paul. He's learnt to imitate the cough of his elder brother! I will never be able to tell their coughs apart again.

Our children learn by copying others, and most of all they copy us. Are you good enough to be copied? Our children will grow up with our attitudes and behaviour. They will model their marriages on the way we treat our wives. They will model their fatherhood on the way we father them. I didn't realize that this copying was taking place until my eldest son was twelve. My awakening came when I recognized my arrogance being used by him towards my wife. Fortunately I realized my mistake just in time, and in the last four years Mary and I have rebuilt the marriage and the family attitudes. Perhaps you too have made a similar mistake. It's not too late to change. Here are the areas where I had to make changes:

Love

I had to show a better example of love towards Mary, so that the family had something better to copy. I had to support her more, encourage her, be more polite and caring. This caused much perplexity to the older boys at first, but as time passed, I was able to explain the changes to them, and ask for their forgiveness for getting it so wrong for so long.

Interest

I had to show more genuine interest in their lives—an interest which was lacking before. I've tried to be more realistic about the difficulties they face and the pressures from their friends. I've learnt to enjoy their company more, and I've been willing, and wanted to spend more time with them.

Tolerance

I've had to learn to be more patient towards them, so that they could learn to be more patient with each other, to others and in time to their own wives.

Sharing

I've learnt to share my world with them. I've shared decisions with the older ones. I haven't been too proud to ask for their advice and to take it on a number of occasions. I've tried to show more love for the younger ones—spending time with them and trying to do some of the more tedious jobs for them that before were all left to Mary. I've tried to get the older boys to do the same, with some success.

Prayer

I've tried to set a better example of prayer with and for them.

Honesty

I've tried to be more honest about myself—confessing my faults and failures, and trying to help them do the same. I've learnt to say sorry to them, and this has encouraged them to do the same in return. I've tried to be more honest about my discipline, and have recognized my failures in this area of my life.

I don't want them to grow up like the old me—that would have been a tragedy, which I only just realized in time. But I believe that the changed me is a better model for them. What about you?

What's the wife's and what's mine?

Bringing up a family is a big responsibility, as many will already know. We have four growing and boisterous boys, and sometimes it seems almost too big a job—not that we are complaining. Our family enrich our lives daily, and we wouldn't be without them.

How can a husband and wife divide the responsibility of bringing up the family, so that both are able to lead creative lives, and neither are worn down by the effort? There are conflicting views today:

* Some think that it's all the wife's responsibility. The husband earns the money and the wife does the rest.
* Some think that the wife cares for the children while they are young and the father has the major part to play when they are older.
* Some think that the workload should be divided equally.
* Some men bring up the family, while the wife earns the money.

How can we work out what a right division is for our marriage and family? These areas need to be considered:

Needs

What are the needs and responsibilities that have to be met? Have you and your wife ever sat down and talked these over?

Division

How are they divided at the moment? Is this a fair division?

Energy

Is either of us getting really worn out by our responsibilities? What can be done about this?

Relaxation

Are we both getting time to relax, or am I getting more than my share?

The Christian man has a different approach to this question. He has to work out the division in the light of God's plan, which is:

Only one head

The husband, as head of the family, carries the ultimate responsibility. This is a heavy position, and leaves no room for arrogance or pride.

Shared responsibility

The husband carries out this responsibility in partnership with his wife. This means that all decisions regarding family life have to be talked over and worked out. Neither partner has the option of saying, 'I leave all that to you.' It's vital that decisions are shared—that way the male and female point of view are brought to bear, and this can only be for the good of the family.

Shared tasks

Within this framework, there is a sharing of practical tasks. The way the work is divided will differ from family to family and will be done for the good of all.

Time alone

We both need opportunities to have time to ourselves, and the spare time available, after all the jobs are done, is shared out. This is essential if we are to become the men and women that God intends.

How does this work out in practice? In our family, it means that sometimes I bath the kids and sometimes Mary does.

Most times she shops, but I do occasionally. She cooks, but we wash up. She irons, and we say 'thank you'. I earn the money which buys us what we need to live, but it's 'our' money, and we spend it together for the good of all.

Is it right for my wife to work while the kids are young?

Many women work today, at all periods of their lives. More and more women take maternity leave from their work and return to their jobs as soon as they can after the birth of their baby. To do this, babies must be left in the care of the family, or of baby minders. The reasons given for leaving their children while they are still young are many:

* We have to pay the mortgage.
* We can't manage on my husband's income.
* I've got my own career to consider.
* It's nice to have the extras.
* My husband is out of work and we desperately need the money.

Like many other marriages, Mary worked as a teacher while our first three were young. It was good to be relieved of the financial pressures of a low income and a large family. It also meant that we were able to have some of the extras, including holidays, which helped me cope with the strain of my job.

But there was a price to pay for the extra money. The family was always under pressure. We were always needing someone to mind the youngest, while the older boys just couldn't be ill, or have time off school. Mary always had to rush away from her school, so that she could meet the children from their school. Day in, day out, this became quite a strain on all of us.

We were beginning to wonder whether it was worth it, and when Mary became pregnant again, we made a decision that she wouldn't work any more, and that she would become a housewife and mother, whatever the financial cost.

It turned out to be the best decision we have ever made. Our marriage and family prospered and our bank balance suffered, but somehow we managed. The benefits far outweighed the strain.

We share this to encourage others to consider the value of the wife being a wife and mother, and being able to fulfil that role, rather than giving in to social or financial pressures to return to work. We would even ask unemployed families to consider it, although we've never faced their pressures, and have no right to insist. As you evaluate this decision, as a husband, it's worth considering what the cost is going to be to you, your wife, and family if she works:

* A baby minder is no substitute for Mum. Why should your child have second best, for the sake of money or career?
* Whoever has long daytime periods with a child will mould the life of that child. Shouldn't you and your wife be doing this? It's your responsibility and privilege, after all.
* You've no control over what habits and practices your child will pick up from a baby minder or family member, however good they are. Shouldn't you be the one exercising the control?
* Your wife is missing out on all the cuddles, gurgles and signs of growth which were meant for her to see and enjoy. Doesn't she have a right to these?

God sees the position of housewife and mother as one of the highest and most important functions in the world. We've got to relearn this truth in a world which sees working wives as the norm, without considering the implications for the children.

How can I help my children?

Fathers should always have this question in the forefront of their minds. Unfortunately I didn't for many years and it was more a question of, 'What's the least I can get away with towards them?' I loved my children, but somehow I never rose above the mediocre towards them.

Over the last four years, I've come to realize that my children are precious, and have been given in trust to me for a few brief years. As I have learnt a new way of treating them, I've had to consider these areas. How would you measure up?

Expectations

I've had to learn to stop forcing my expectations on them, and to let them be themselves. I try to encourage them in their school work and their social awareness, but at the same time I keep a check on my encouragements, so that I'm not pushing them in the direction that I want them to go. It's a difficult balance, but I believe it will lead them into mature adulthood.

Friendship

I want to finish up with four adult men who are my friends and who enjoy my company, so I've got to be prepared to share their world and to let them share mine. This takes commitment on both sides, but the end result will be well worth the effort.

Faith

I want my children to share my faith in God, but they need to know him for themselves. So I let them see how my faith works—both the highs and the lows. I don't pretend before them that it's all easy or that I never have doubts. I try to give them as much information as possible, so that they can make their decisions. This is a father's job, whether he believes in God or not. We do not have the right to force our faith, or our non-faith, on our children.

Lifestyle

I long for my sons to be manly: men with hearts of compassion, men who can express their feelings, men who can live with strength and weakness, men who will be good husbands and fathers. They are going to learn these things by studying and copying my lifestyle and behaviour. So I have a responsibility to make sure that I am right in these areas of my life.

Discipline

My sons need to learn about discipline. Not just the discipline that involves punishment, but also self-discipline and self-control. They will learn this from a loving father, who disciplines them with fairness, but who also disciplines himself. This is another responsibility which I need to take into account.

Stickability

My commitment to my children must be total. No matter what they do, or don't do, they need to know that my love and trust cannot be broken. Sometimes it's tempting to give up, but on these occasions I remember that God must often feel the same about me, and yet he continues to love and support me. Surely I can do the same for my children.

Apology

I'm not always right, and sometimes I have to say 'sorry' to my children and ask for their forgiveness. This does not always come easily to me, but they will never learn the meaning and value of forgiveness if they never have to give it themselves.

Do I give my children enough time?

Children need time from us, and they often want it at awkward moments. Last night, I got in from a long hard trip. I was so tired, that all I wanted to do was to sit in the armchair. As I sat there, my six-year-old appeared beside me, complete with trainers and coat. 'Dad, you promised to come out into the garden with me tonight. Are you ready?'

In the same way, when I met my thirteen-year-old from school recently, he dropped his schoolbag in the middle of the pavement and regardless of the chaos he was causing, showed me his maths book with great pride. He had no intention of waiting until it suited me to look!

How can we be sure we are giving our children the time they need and deserve, and at the same time support our wives and stay sane?

They have a right to it

By giving time to our children, we are giving them ourselves, which is the most precious gift we have to give. But they don't have to earn the right to our time. They have a right to it simply because they are our children. If we were not prepared to give them time, we should not have had them in the first place. This is the starting point from which we work out how much time we should spend with them. Again and again I have to remind myself that my children are my children through my choice. Should you be remembering this next time you get home from work? By the way—I did go out in the garden that night!

At the time of their choosing

We often impose our adult timetable on the world of our

children and forget the immediacy of their needs. If we keep saying 'not now but later', then they will stop wanting to be with us, and we will lose many precious moments. The wise father knows that he has sometimes to say 'not now', but he also makes sure that he doesn't say it too often, and that he's also very willing to drop all that he is doing, so that he can enjoy 'now' with his children. Is this your attitude?

They have a right to good time

So often we give our children time that we've no other use for, but this isn't good enough. They have a right to quality time—time we would rather use for ourselves. They want some of our weekend, some of our night off, some of our hobby time. The wise parent will recognize this and give freely. Children do recognize when they're getting valuable time, and so it becomes more special to them.

They have a right to family time

A family shows what it values most by the way it treats things. Every family has to eat, and this can be special time for *all* the children to share with you and you with them.

Check it out

These questions will challenge your time priorities.

* When did you last spend an hour with each member of your family?
* What did you do?
* When are you planning to do it again?

Is my discipline fair?

A father cannot avoid discipline. If he does, then his family becomes little more than a collection of individuals, each doing their own thing under the same roof.

But how do we exercise discipline, so that all involved feel that justice is being done?

Start with ourselves

If we are not leading disciplined lives, then we will never achieve fair discipline with our children. For example, I like buying things, and as an adult I'm in a position to have whatever I can afford. The children want everything, but cannot afford it. Is it right that I should be uncontrolled in my spending, while expecting them to manage on very limited resources? Can I discipline their wants, if they see that I always have what I want?

Are you disciplined in your daily life? Who checks you when you get out of control?

Do it out of genuine love

Discipline must come from a loving heart, not an angry one. If we discipline from love, then discipline will always bring us back to love, not to resentment.

Recently David (fifteen) wanted to go on a night hike. I wasn't satisfied that it was organized well enough to guarantee his safety and said so. He was very angry and stormed off. Eventually I said, in exasperation, 'Look, perhaps I love you too much to want to see you get hurt!' I don't think he had ever seen it this way, and it eased the situation.

Recognize that there are different levels

My children range from two to fifteen and I've learnt that not only must my discipline relate to their age, but also to their temperament. Young ones might stop at a command, a smack or being sent to bed, but that's no good with the older ones. I also know that one of my older ones never responds to being shouted at, while the other probably will!

Are you matching discipline to age and temperament?

Make sure they know the rules

Do your children know what you expect in terms of behaviour, and what the consequences will be of disobedience?

Be fair

If the rules and punishments are clear, do you implement them fairly? Children get very perplexed and annoyed at inconsistency in adults.

Discipline with mercy

It isn't always necessary to implement the full discipline, even though we have the right to do so. We can always exercise a little leniency, and this will sometimes achieve more than full discipline. Do you know when to be lenient?

Think beyond your generation

The Bible tells us that we should teach a child in the way he should go. As we discipline our children, we are helping them set the standards for their own lives, and they will treat your grandchildren in much the same way that you treat and discipline them. That's why it's so important for us to get it right.

Forgive and forget

Once a child has been disciplined, then that should be the end of the matter. There is no room for malice, or grudge bearing. Discipline should be the way back to love and peace, and it's vital that our children know that this is our way. Do your children know this of you?

What happens if children 'go wrong'?

Most parents worry about their children getting into some sort of trouble. We can take as much care as we can at home, but outside of our environment they are subject to many other pressures, which they might find it hard to withstand. The sorts of things we worry about are:

* Trouble with the police, through something like shoplifting.
* Involvement with crime.
* Heavy drinking.
* Getting into bad company.
* Becoming pregnant, or making a girl pregnant.

Most of us face these concerns, and sadly children of every age and background do get into trouble. When they do, we experience a mixture of emotions—shame, anger, guilt, embarrassment—but they need our help. What can we do?

Know we're not alone

It's easy for us to think that it's only our child who is in trouble, and that we're the only parents who are trying to work things out. But many parents will understand our difficulties, having been through them personally.

Recognize that our feelings are involved

We men can be very bad at handling feelings and emotions, but we would do well to recognize that they are very much involved in the situation. Facing this truth will help us be more realistic in our approach to our child.

Stand by them

More than anything else, our children need to know that nothing can break the love that we have for them. We may have to appear in court with them, face other people with them, even visit them in prison—but we must never desert them. They need to know that we are truly a friend in need. Are you prepared to make this commitment, or are you so ashamed or embarrassed that you want to desert them? It isn't going to be easy to stand by them.

Welcome them home

The Bible tells a story of a hurt father. His son takes his inheritance, leaves home and spends it all on riotous living. But when a famine comes and the money is gone, he is reduced to very low circumstances. He returns home, expecting to meet a harsh and judging father, instead of which the father welcomes him home with joy. He is so pleased to have his son back. You may be a hurt father, but are you a welcoming one? Is the welcome mat always out in your home and your heart? Are you on the lookout for the 'I'm sorry, can I come home' signal, no matter what your son or daughter has done, how much they have hurt, how desperate the mistake, how deep your anger?

Face facts

Love is not a doormat. Sometimes love needs to be tough. Once the child is welcomed home, it's necessary to look into the reasons for the mistake, and the consequences, so that it doesn't happen again. Otherwise, we are just ignoring our responsibility. But we're not to lecture our child. Facts can only be faced if there's a willingness for both sides to examine themselves. We're not wholly without blame when a child gets into difficulty. Are we willing to let our hearts be examined too?

Be understanding

The world of young people is extremely confused. Values are very fluid and pressures can be very hard to withstand. Sometimes they have been tricked into doing wrong, or it's happened through inexperience. Sometimes it's a cry for attention, or for help. Are you willing to try and understand their world, and to see things from their point of view?

Assist the healing

After the mistake needs to come the healing—undoing the damage, making restitution, healing of relationships, the making of a new beginning. Are you the sort of parent who will try and see the way to healing, and do everything in your power to help it come?

In God, there is always forgiveness and new beginnings. Many parents have come into a real living faith when faced with a youngster in trouble.

What happens when my children get under my skin?

We're a very happy family. There are six of us and, although we all have different needs, we seem to get along happily together most of the time.

Occasionally, however, for any of a number of reasons, one of the children will really irritate Mary or myself. Sometimes there's an obvious reason—like we're very tired, or under pressure of some sort. Sometimes they are tired or under pressure, and get very edgy. Sometimes there doesn't seem to be an obvious reason at all.

At these times, feelings run very high, tempers flare and things are said which aren't really meant. How should we react? What should we do?

Get a hold of ourselves

First and foremost, it's vital that we keep control of how we are feeling about the situation. We cannot ignore our feelings, and we would be foolish to do so, but we should have the maturity to keep them under control and to recognize that our children are not always able to do the same. They are depending on us to find a way out of the situation, so we need to keep a cool head.

Do you? Or do you just shout or hit and leave it at that?

Share feelings

It's good if we can share how we are feeling with our wives. This prevents feelings being bottled up inside us. It takes courage to share these feelings.

Look for a possible fault in ourselves

When the children irritate, it isn't always their fault. Is there anything we are doing which is making them irritable? Is there something going on in our life which is worrying us, and we're taking it out on them?

Listen

If it's something in the children themselves which is causing irritation, we need to learn to listen carefully to them, so that we can identify the cause. Last week, John was in a bad mood and he really got under my skin. At first I managed to keep my feelings in, but eventually I couldn't stand any more, and I exploded. Then I began to look for the cause—and found it in his homework. He had too much and didn't know how to handle it. So I began to help him and all the irritation went. Our children's world is very confused and fluid, and any one of a number of things could be causing them to react.

Give attention

Sometimes the children are irritable because they want more of our attention than they are getting already. Perhaps we need to examine how we are using our time with them. Do they need more? Can we manage just a little more love and care?

Endure

If, despite all our efforts, our children continue to get under our skin, then all we can do is to wait and endure. Bad times pass and moments for reconciliation do come. Parents who truly love their children have to have the gift of endurance. Will you endure? When a chance comes for a new beginning, are you ready to make the first move, or are you too proud? Our children depend on us being willing to make the openings so that they can start again.

How do we let go of our children?

I can still remember the day I left home. At the age of eighteen, I was going off to university. I woke up to see Mum coming into my room to wish me a good trip. I noticed that she was crying, although I didn't know why. Now I've got children of my own, I can understand only too well.

We all want our children to become independent human beings, making their own decisions in their own right. To achieve this, we have to learn to let them go their own way.

Always our children

In a very real sense, our children will always belong to us. Our care and concern for them will never end, and they are entitled to a home with us for as long as they need or want it. We have to learn the art of letting them go, but this can only be done within the context of a permanent place in our home and in our hearts. There is a danger in not letting go, but there is an equal danger in being so determined that they be independent, that we almost drive them away from us.

What kind of independence?

As we learn to let them go, we must be letting them go into the right pattern. They need to be independent in their own right, secure in their own personality and loved by their parents. We lose something when they leave our protection, but it's a great privilege to see them becoming mature people. Are you able to see it this way?

They have the right

Our children have the right to independence, and they have to look for it themselves. Part of the art of loving is to let them begin to explore independence—letting them go places on their own, to learn from other people, to read and think. As we find our children wanting more independence, we have to make careful judgements. If we deny them the chance of increasing independence as they grow up, not only are we denying them an essential right, but it will certainly rebound on us later. Are you letting your children explore their independence?

Letting go in love

We conceived our children in love, nurtured them in love, and now we must let them go with that same love. Letting go is one of life's great experiences, and we need to see it in a positive light.

Many blessings

There are great benefits in having children who are independent and people in their own right. My eldest son, who is quite independent now, is a really good friend of mine. He's become a help and an advisor as well. This is greatly enriching my life and I hope that it will continue and that we will be really good friends in his adult life.

Tough for Mum

Our wives find the letting go process much harder, and we need to help them see the necessity and the joy of it. Not only do we have to reassure them that this is a right and healthy process—we also have to help them find new outlets for their energies now that the children have grown up. Husbands have to be very careful and sensitive during this period.

Are you doing all you can to help your wife?

What about children of a former marriage?

With a rising divorce rate, more and more men are having to face up to this issue. It can get complicated:

* There can be children from his former marriage.
* There can be children from his wife's former marriage.
* There can be children from the new marriage.
* There are parents from the former marriages involved as well.

How can a man manage under these circumstances?

A father is a father

No matter what has happened, a man cannot ignore the fact that he is the father of a child. He must have concern for children of a former marriage, even if the practical caring has passed to another person. He must have equal concern for the children of a new marriage. It's not an easy path to tread.

New patterns

There have to be new ways of relating to children of a former marriage. Things cannot go on as before—this is part of the price of a broken marriage. The new patterns need careful working out—between the man, his former wife and his current one. It takes courage and time to sort this out.

Much hurt

The children of a former marriage will be hurt and confused by the divorce and change of relationships. They might blame the father and might not want to see him. It's no good getting angry about this—after all there might be some truth in what they feel. The father needs to go on loving and caring, whatever the cost to him. Only God can teach us how to handle this kind of hurt, and many a man has turned to him at this time.

Let go

If a woman remarries, then the new husband must be allowed to have the major say with the children. A father is always a father, but he needs the wisdom and grace to let his children pass into the care of another man, without abandoning responsibility for them. This is another very difficult balance to get right.

New dad

A man might marry again and find that he's become 'Dad' to children of whom he isn't the natural father. Working this out and caring for these children will be a major responsibility.

A man who remarries needs the greatest sensitivity and wisdom towards all the children involved. The children are already badly hurt by the divorce. If the father doesn't get things right, they will be hurt even more.

What if we can't have children?

Some couples choose not to have children. Other couples decide they do want children and have very little trouble. Some, however, long for children, but for some reason they cannot conceive, or each pregnancy ends in a miscarriage.

Couples in this last category are under great pressure. They live in a society where most people have children, and they can feel a tremendous sense of inadequacy and a great sorrow. The wife feels that her creative instincts are not being fulfilled, and a husband feels that his very manliness is being challenged.

The Bible talks of these external and internal pressures. Hannah was desperately sad because she was infertile, and she was very fortunate in having a very caring husband. He comforted her with these words: 'Don't I mean more to you than ten sons?' (1 Samuel 1:8).

This statement might not look very positive, but it was all I could think of to comfort Mary when one of our babies died, and it seemed an appropriate thing to say.

Is there anything a man can do when he is facing this situation?

Know that marriage is more than children

We marry our wives because we love them—not for the children they might bear us. As a couple, we need to keep remembering this truth. Our wives are precious to us for who they are, not for what they can or cannot do. Our manliness does not depend on our ability to create children, but on the way we are and the way we behave.

Face the feelings

There are many feelings surrounding this issue and they need to be faced, not ignored. Are you prepared to be honest and face them? Can you talk to your wife about how you really feel? Do you have a close friend who will listen?

Care a lot

Our wives will need extra care and support from us. Are you prepared to give the extra?

Redirect energy

There is no substitute for a family, but perhaps it's possible to redirect that creative energy.

Pray

Issues like this often bring us to the point of prayer. Sometimes God anwers our 'why?' and sometimes he doesn't. But through prayer he is able to give us the courage to carry on, and the strength to support our wives.

SECTION FOUR

Work

Why work?

'What are you going to do when you leave school?'

This is the question everyone asks my eldest son, because it is assumed that he will both want and need a paid job. Adults behave in exactly the same way. Whenever I meet a man, and we get talking, one of the first things I ask is, 'What do you do for a living?' I expect him to have a paid job, or at least to have had one. These are not bad expectations. Paid work brings many benefits to us:

* It's a means of supporting ourselves and our families.
* It gives a degree of financial independence, so that we can have the extra things that aren't strictly necessities, if we want them.
* It helps us feel valuable. By having a paid job, we feel that we are worth something to the society in which we live.
* If gives us our place in that society, and so we feel comfortable.
* It gives us a chance to meet and to be with other people, which we might not have if we didn't have paid work.
* It gives a timetable for our daily lives, which we both value and need.
* Underneath it all, paid work satisfies something deep within our masculine personalities. When we are in paid work, we feel 'right', we feel 'men'.

We are foolish to lose these benefits by not having a paid job, if one is available. But for millions today, paid work is not available, and so many of these benefits are denied them. This situation isn't helped by the general belief that we have a right to paid work, and that anyone who doesn't have a job is a scrounger. As a result of this attitude, many men are left feeling isolated, lonely and cheated. They feel of no value, and their lives lack direction.

God has given us both the skills to support ourselves, and the desire to do so. That's why we feel right when we're in paid work. But he doesn't value a man by the paid work he does.

In God's sight, every man is unique and valuable for who he is, rather than for what he does. This is a vital lesson for all, whether with or without paid work. It puts work in its right place as part, but only part, of a man's total experience.

God has a plan and a purpose for every life. This plan can be fulfilled whether there is paid work or not. Putting God at the centre of our lives, rather than work, brings all our experiences into the right perspective.

We've no excuse for not taking a paid job, if there is one to suit us. But with so many men out of paid work, it's time for a reassessment of the place of paid work in the total experience of life. We need new understandings, which will help the millions without paid work to rediscover their place and value to our society.

Am I paid what I'm worth?

I used to work in a factory, and pay was one of our favourite topics for discussion. Generally we were always looking for more pay. On the shop floor, the unions put steady pressure on management for increases, while in the offices, there were constant discussions with the senior management. In fact, we weren't too badly paid. No one ever dropped dead from starvation, and most of us managed to run a car and pay the bills. But we always thought that we were worth more. What we really wanted was access to many of the luxury goods on sale in the shops, and which in consumer society we were being told we couldn't manage without: videos, better cars, holidays abroad, and so on. A better salary would allow us to have these things, as well as improving our status in the eyes of other men.

We were always after more, but never considered these questions:

Am I worth what I'm paid?

Before we consider whether we're being treated fairly, do we treat our employer fairly? Do we do a fair day's work for our pay? Do we cheat our employer by being late, by stealing, by not giving all of our talents to the job?

Who pays for my increase?

If we think we're worth more, who will suffer so that we can have our increase? Sometimes it's all tied up with profitability, but there are some cases where we get richer at the expense of the poor, who get poorer.

Am I concerned just for myself?

We can be very selfish about our worth and our pay. Are we as keen to consider the rights of others who may be paid very poorly, or who work in very poor conditions, or who have no recourse to union or government help?

Bearing these questions in mind, how can we be sure that we are getting a fair return for our labours? There is nothing wrong with asking this question, as long as we're prepared to face the implications of it as outlined already.

Be involved

Most workplaces have methods of negotiating pay and conditions. If we want to be sure that we are getting a right return, then we need to be actively involved, rather than just leaving it to others to negotiate on our behalf.

Be aware

We need to be aware of what others are being paid in our workplace for doing a similar job, and what others are being paid in other places for similar jobs. This way, we'll be realistic in our expectations.

Be realistic

Most of us would settle for a massive pay rise each year, but can our workplace afford it? Try and get some idea of what might be affordable at the current time. This will make a good starting point.

Look to others

Are there people in our workplace who are being treated unfairly? Are we as concerned for them as for ourselves?

Be satisfied

Maybe we are being paid what we are worth. Act as a man who is content with his pay and conditions, rather than being ungrateful or full of dissent.

Could I do better?

The factory where I worked was on a large industrial estate. There were other factories around us, and men would move from place to place to improve their circumstances. One of my friends decided to move. He applied for a job elsewhere, got it, and started to work out his three month's notice. He seemed happy to move, but as the time to leave drew near, he became very quiet. He began to think of the friends he would lose, of having to start all over again in a new job. Conditions in our plant weren't bad and the pay was reasonable. With only two weeks left before he was to leave, he turned the new job down and stayed with us. The only comment he made was, 'I had too much to lose, Jim.'

Many men could do better financially by moving, and there's no reason why we shouldn't do better, but we must be prepared to face the hard questions:

* Am I moving just for the money? Is that a good enough reason for moving?
* What will I lose if I move? Friends? A job I know I can handle? Conditions I like? Will a bigger salary compensate for these? Will I be able to make new friends?
* Are there implications for my family if I change jobs? Will we have to move house or school? Will new working hours mean I'm away from home more? Will I have to work much harder for better money, and so have less time for my wife?

Not everyone is looking for more money, but some men want to be able to use the gifts they have more effectively, and in this sense we want to do better. What can we do?

* We could move to a more challenging job in another place, where we will enjoy the stimulus of new friends, new pressures, new opportunities. In my profession, this is an accepted practice, and I personally enjoy it.
* We might be able to make more of the job we've got. Perhaps discussions with the person to whom we are directly responsible will bring this about.

Perhaps, for some of us, the challenge to do better in our job is a reprimand. Maybe we haven't been giving our best to our work, our colleagues or our employer. Ask yourself:

* Do I keep good time at work?
* Do I cheat—bring things home?
* Do I use my talents to the full for my work, or do I just do as little as I can to get by on?
* Can I be trusted to do the job I've been assigned to?

Christian men work for a higher authority and are answerable to God for effort, potential and honest commitment in the workplace. We face these questions:

* Is this God's place for me at this time? It is our responsibility to ensure that we always know the answer to this question.
* Is my work fulfilling me as a person? God is always looking to fulfil our potential, and if we're finding work unfulfilling, we either need to change our job or our attitude.

How do I get to the top?

Men are very competitive. Most of us want to get on, and some of us want to get to the very top of our area of work or profession.

There's nothing wrong with wanting to get to the top in any job or profession. God has given to some the desire to be there, and they can only be fully themselves when they are there. What can be wrong, however, is our behaviour once we are in a top position. There are many pressures at the top which can lead us astray:

* The need to be successful.
* The strain on the family.
* Very long hours of high concentration.
* The temptation to abuse the position—dealing corruptly and misusing power and influence.
* Misusing the trust and loyalty of others.
* The desire to look after ourselves.

We don't have to give in to these pressures. We don't have to become corrupt, cheats, liars, ruthless and uncompassionate men. We can get to the top and give of our very best for the good of others as well as ourselves. But to do this, we have to face some hard questions:

Why do I want to get to the top?

This is not a question that can be answered quickly or easily. But a man should only want to get to the top because he believes that only there can he fulfil his true potential as a human being, and because he genuinely believes that once there, his actions will benefit many people and not just himself.

How will I get there?

The methods a man uses to get to the top will reveal to others his reasons for wanting to be there. Are you:

* Prepared to trample on others, as long as you get on?
* Willing to compromise at every point to get there?
* Prepared to work hard and conscientiously?
* Loyal to your colleagues and your employer?
* Willing to sacrifice your family life and your leisure time?
* Looking to benefit by the mistakes of others?

Am I a man of good will?

Does promotion matter more to you than being a man of good will and principle, compassionate and caring towards others?

Am I an honest dealer?

Is everything you do above board? Do others know that this is the way you work? Do you know the difference between friendship and undue influence, through the use of gifts?

Do I know the dangers of my position?

Those at the top have great power. Do you know how dangerous such power is? Do you use it with care, and for the good of all who work under you? Are you ever vindictive in the use of power? Are you aware of the temptations that surround you? What steps have you taken to protect yourself against them?

Do I make the effort?

No one ever got to the place where they are at their best without hard work. Do you work hard? Are you prepared for the effort that goes with great responsibility?

Can I take the knocks?

There are many setbacks on the way to the top and many pressures once there. Can you take the strain?

Are my values right?

Do you value your health? Do you value your marriage and family? Will you ensure that they get a fair share of your time?

Are my morals strong and clear?

A man at the top needs to know what he believes and why he believes it. Have you got your thinking clear?

Can I be honest *and* successful?

A friend of mine runs a building business. He is known as a committed Christian man, and his business principles are very strict. He always keeps his word, and will have nothing to do with anything that is dubious. He does a very good job and works very hard. Over the years his business has flourished on these very principles, and now he is a very successful man. He has maintained his integrity and prospered in a very competitive and commercial environment.

Some successful people are known to be dishonest, and others have an aura of dishonesty about them, but many people—Christians and non-Christians—have been both successful and honest. It's a combination which is very appealing to consumers in any place and form. We don't have to be dishonest to achieve. But what kind of man do we have to be, to be honest and successful? We need a mixture of moral principles and practical abilities:

Integrity

An honest man must be known for his honesty. He must be willing to stick to his principles, even when they appear to place him at a disadvantage.

Discipline

A successful man needs to lead a disciplined life. He needs to work hard, but also needs to allow time for family and for relaxation.

Compassion

Compassion and understanding stop successful men from becoming hard and ruthless.

Flexibility

Successful men are those who are able to see that a particular course of action needs changing, and are willing to adapt quickly to changing circumstances.

Toughness

A man who wants to get on will always come up against hard knocks, failures and setbacks. He must have a determination to overcome them, rather than to give in to them.

Sense of humour

A man needs to be able to laugh at things, himself and others—otherwise he runs the risk of becoming unstable in his personality.

Christian men have one more principle to add—obedience. We do not think in terms of success or failure. We are just obedient to God, and then let him open the way for us. With obedience in our hearts, we can be as successful as any man, but we won't let it go to our heads. We will see it as part of God's purpose for us, and will give him all the glory.

What do those at work think of me?

When I worked as a temporary planning engineer, I was with a team of men. Our boss was trying to get promotion in the factory, but he never seemed to make it, so we pitied him. One of the senior engineers was always trying to give contracts to people who would give him nice presents at Christmas, so we were rather cynical about him. Our filing clerk was so miserable, that we were always glad when he was off sick. Yet despite these attitudes, we worked well together. I had no idea what they thought of me, until I came to leave. I went to see the boss, and he said, 'We were all a bit worried here when we knew you were coming. We didn't know what a trainee vicar would be like. We imagined that you would be really solemn and carry a Bible!'

It never occurred to me that my colleagues were weighing me up—perhaps it was good for me that I didn't. By the time I found out, it didn't matter, because by then I had formed good relationshps with them. It's important to feel good at work, but do we really know what our colleagues think of us? What would your friends say about you? Try these questions:

* Do my colleagues and workmates like me as a person, rather than just get on with me as a colleague?
* Do they like the way I work? Am I reliable and can I be counted on?
* Are they loyal to me? As a manager or employer, will my employees make extra effort when the pressure is on? As a worker, will my colleagues cover for me if I need a bit of extra help, or a little time off?
* How much would they value me if I stepped outside the accepted patterns and ways of doing things?

* When I'm late or wrong, do my friends stand by me?
* If I've made mistakes in relationships at work, will my fellow workers let me put them right?
* Am I known as one who tries to help my fellow workers, or am I known as an awkward customer?
* How do they react if they know I'm a Christian? What difference does being a Christian make to me in the workplace?

Maybe these questions have made you aware of shortcomings at your workplace, either in your own behaviour, or in the behaviour of others. If this is the case, them some new beginnings are necessary. Are you willing to let them start with and in you?

Do I take work home with me?

Like many men, I used to work overtime if I had the opportunity, and since this was quite often, it affected my home life. I was too tired to listen to Mary as she shared her day, and I didn't want to go out to church activities, especially if they required me to think. This kind of thing is far from unusual, and can be lived with. The problems really arise when men can't leave work alone when they are home. This damages home life, as well as making them tired and ineffective in their daily working lives.

Some men are under such pressure to achieve, that they must work when they get home. Others don't want to leave work alone, and use it as an excuse to escape from family responsibilities, or from facing the truth about a breaking marriage.

All of us need to develop some basic ground rules which will help us live at work with our home and at home with our work. They will vary from person to person, of course, but here are some questions which could help in the formulation of these basic rules:

* Is the homework necessary to do my job properly, or am I being inefficient in my working day?
* Is my employer expecting too much of me? Should he be thinking of restructuring my work, so that it fits the time available?
* Is homework a sign of my weakness? If a sound home life is vital to a man's working life, shouldn't I have the courage to say 'no' to homework?
* Is my homework just an ego trip? Am I just trying to make myself look important?
* Does my homework make me more or less efficient? Do I

arrive at work less fresh as I've been working at home? Would I be more creative if I had some hours without thinking of work?
* Does the need to do homework reflect the fact that I'm not disciplined enough in the way I handle my time and my workload?
* Is my homework damaging my health, my wife, my family, or my leisure time?
* Is my homework spoiling my sleep? (Many of the world's greatest men refused to lose their sleep. If you're losing yours, you're out of step with them.)
* Is my homework just a temporary measure to relieve a backlog of work?

There's obviously a balance to be worked out here for those of us who do take more than just the memories of work home with us. If homework is essential to the job, then we need a very high level of self-discipline, to ensure that the home and family life do not suffer. If the discipline is lacking, then eventually everything will be spoilt—our health, our marriage and family, and ultimately our work. We will burn out, and God never intended this to happen to anyone.

The Christian man can face as much homework as his secular colleagues. The pressures and the questions are the same. But we have our reference point in God, and we can look to him for leading, guidance and discipline. He has our best in mind, and the best can never be the wrecking of our health, home and working lives.

Do I cheat at work?

In the factory where I worked, it was estimated that about
£200,000 of stock was going out through the gates each year
in the boots of our cars. It wasn't just bits and pieces either—
some were arranging for quite large amounts of goods to go
home. Everyone was involved, from senior management to
the shop floor.

It was hard to know where to draw the line on this matter.
A lot of the stuff was technically scrap, or of little value. Some
of it was perks, given in lieu of extra pay, or willingness to
work the extra bit of time. As one manager said, 'We could
stop it, but it's a relatively small sum, and it keeps the
workforce happy.'

But at what point does this kind of thing become theft?
Where should we take a stand?

This isn't the only side to the question of cheating. We
have to face the fact that sometimes we don't give all of our
talent and effort to our job, even though we're being paid to
do so. Is taking stuff home in the boot of the car any more
stealing than failing to give our full skills to our jobs?

There's another grey area to be considerd. When orders
and contracts are placed, how far can we accept presents—
meals, Christmas gifts and so on—from contractors, as part
of the social order of the commercial world, and at what point
are we being unduly influenced by a particular contractor
who wants our work, and thinks that a few well-placed gifts
will incline us to his quotation?

Cheating at work isn't an easy issue to resolve, and it's
difficult to set objective standards because circumstances
differ. There are, however, some general guidelines.

Be alert

We should never stop checking our own actions and thoughts. It's so easy to slip into cheating ways without noticing.

Question

We must be very questioning about our motives, and those of others. We're not to have an attitude of distrust, but we must always be prepared to challenge what's being said or done, so that there is no room for even thoughts of cheating.

Don't compromise

We should not adjust our ways to the standards of others, but use them as a measure of our own.

Be aware of the difficulty

It's important to recognize the difficulty of this area. Some would like to make all issues black and white, but many issues at work will not resolve themselves so clearly. Sometimes a lot of thought is needed to get at the truth.

Never rest

We should be constantly looking to improve our standards, rather than settling for them as they are. If we adopt this attitude, we're less likely to slip up.

Christian men do not have a monopoly when it comes to a desire to be honest, but we do have a very objective standard in Christ's life and teachings. We are challenged by all the above questions, and we also face these:

* How does what I'm doing fit in with what Jesus teaches in the Bible?
* What do I do if I've got my standards wrong? How do I change them to fit his teaching?
* Am I prepared to let him change me so that my standards might improve?

What happens if I have problems?

We all have problems which affect our work from time to time. They are usually difficult to sort out, and are made harder for us by the tough-guy image, which tries to tell us that we are totally competent at all things.

Home problems

Trouble with our marriage, or with our children, makes us less effective at work. Maybe we withdraw into ourselves, become tense, start to forget simple things. We probably won't talk about it, so our colleagues will assume that we're losing our grip on our job.

Illness

Long-term illness can cause many problems at work. We lose the continuity of our job through absence and we may feel we are putting pressure on our colleagues. It may also cause us to be short tempered with a customer, forget an appointment, or make a misjudgement.

Too big a job

If we are in a job that is too tough for us, or is beyond our capability, then sooner or later we're going to have problems—with ourselves, our colleagues, or our customers.

Not good enough

We can be ineffective or incompetent in our job, which will lead to all kinds of problems, and could result in us losing our job.

Relationships

We find that we can't get on with those we work with, and this corrodes the atmosphere of the workplace.

Oversight

We can all make mistakes, but the problem for us at work is that we have to live through and with them.

Crime

Most of us face temptation to cheat or steal at work. Some may even be involved in serious thefts and frauds.

What can we do when we have problems at work?

Recognize the problem

Men don't like facing hard truths about themselves and their environments. But the first step to problem-solving is to recognize that there is a problem to be overcome.

Face responsibility

Some problems are our fault and some are not. We need to sort them out, and act where we feel that we have some responsibility. It they are outside our control, then we must put up with them, try to talk them over with those who have the power to act, or change jobs.

Share

Problems are not meant to be a solitary experience. We all need someone who will give us time, and who will listen. Often it's in speaking them out loud to another, that we begin to see the solution. Then we need to act.

Problems can teach us a lot about ourselves, and who our true friends are, as well as making us more understanding of the problems of others. In my experience, the finest problem-solver in the world is Jesus Christ. He doesn't take all our problems away—that would be treating us like children— but he uses them to help us fulfil our true potential.

SECTION FIVE

No Work

How can I survive without a job?

All of us were paid on a Friday in my factory, and I always felt good on Friday evening. There was something very satisfying about bringing home my pay. Paid work brings many tangible benefits—I could pay the bills, support the family, and even buy some luxury items. But bringing home the pay touches something deeper than tangible things. I couldn't put this feeling clearly into words, but somehow I felt very manly, very right about things.

When a man has no paid work, he loses both the tangible benefits, and more seriously the intangible ones. He doesn't feel right about his life. He is often plunged into uncertainty, financial hardship, depression and a sense of worthlessness. Most men are convinced that they must have a paid job and search hard for one. When they are unsuccessful, they can easily become bitter and depressed.

In our current world economy, it's apparent that many men are going to have to spend many years without paid work. Somehow we have to find a way of living without paid work which will not result in our feeling bitter and depressed. The key is to challenge the whole concept of paid work. It has become the main aim of the lives of so many men, yet it was never meant to be that central. Employment is much wider, and life much bigger, than paid work. We don't have to be in paid work to feel right about ourselves, or to feel that we are worth something to society. It's time for a radical change of approach, and it can begin in the attitudes of those without paid work. We must begin to look for:

* A sense of meaning in life outside of paid work.
* Time to be with other men. This is vital to us as men, and

helps us keep a balance in our outlook.
* Deeper fulfilment in our home life and in all relationships.
* A way of serving the community. Serving others is one of the best ways of feeling right about ourselves, and feeling that we have something to offer society.
* Opportunity to harness creative skills. Looking for chances to be creative is one of the deepest expressions of human nature. Paid work doesn't always give this opportunity.
* Opportunities to develop other interests. As we become interested in other things, so our own problems are kept in perspective.

All men without paid work—whether Christian or not—face the same uncertainties, worries and feelings of worthlessness. Sometimes Christian men also have to cope with feelings that God has let them down. But we do have extra resources:

* A fixed reference point in our faith in God. He is the centre of our lives, not paid work.
* A conviction that God has a plan for our lives, no matter how things may look on the surface. A period of unpaid time is not an accident as far as we are concerned.
* The understanding that God can and will provide for every need.

Why can't I get a job?

When a man loses his paid employment, he nearly always looks for another job. Sometimes this proves an easy search, but in times of high unemployment, it can be a real struggle. When we can't get paid work, we make all sorts of excuses. These are the common ones:

* It's an unfair world. Others are just luckier than I am.
* If only I were someone else, or somewhere else, I would be lucky too.
* It's the government's fault that I can't get a job.
* I'm past it now.
* It's a waste of time even going for interviews. There are hundreds of others after the same jobs. What hope have I got?

These excuses may make us feel better, but they do not help us understand why we can't get a job. The hard truth is often that nobody wants what we have to offer. Once we face this truth, then we have to take an honest look at ourselves, perhaps for the first time.

Are you prepared to take an honest look at yourself? These are the sorts of questions which need to be faced:

* What am I really like as a person? Are there things about me that make others dislike me? What are my strong points? How do I behave?
* How do I cope with pressure? How am I coping with the pressures that this situation is creating?
* Am I prepared to be honest about my feelings of depression, frustration, loneliness, anger, despair, hopelessness?

* I've pitied other men in this position—now how does it really feel?
* Are there others that can help me think and feel my way through this time? Am I prepared to share with them, or am I too proud?
* What direction should my life take now that I've failed to get a paid job? Should I go on applying? Should I move? Should I retrain? Should I build a life without paid work?
* Are there any openings that I've missed—government schemes, friends with contacts?
* What have I got to offer an employer? (Make a list, including the positives and the negatives.)
* Has paid work become too important to me? Is is damaging other parts of my life?
* Have I made work the basis of my dignity as a man? Is this right?
* Is my lifestyle being modelled on that of people in paid work, rather than looking for a style which will suit my unpaid working situation?
* Are there things I can do now that I have no paid work, that I couldn't do before?
* What can I offer the community that I couldn't offer before?
* How can I make sure that I still get relaxation, breaks and holidays?
* Does my wife share my fears and hopes? Do I share hers?
* Am I passing on to my children honesty and integrity, the willingness to adapt?
* Is it time to think through issues of faith and belief, as many men do at times of crisis?

How can I cope with feeling useless?

When Mary was having our third child, I was with her all the time, and this was a marvellous experience. But occasionally I had to leave her, so that she could have some treatment. During those periods, as I stood in the waiting room, I felt completely useless. I wasn't where I wanted to be, and I felt that I wasn't in control of the situation.

Men with no paid work often have this same feeling of uselessness and frustration. They feel that they don't matter to anyone, and that they are out of control of their own lives. This is a very tough feeling to live with, and as well as spoiling his own life, it can ruin a man's marriage and home life. How can we live with feeling useless?

Be positive

What things have we got to contribute to society, despite not having a paid job? Possibilities include a balanced personality, a secure marriage with cared for children, compassion, skills and talents, a willingness to serve others, a sense of humour, compassion for the needy and good health. No price tag can be placed on any of these things.

Accept the new lifestyle

We feel useless because we are looking back at the paid work days. We must learn to enter the non-paid work situation with a positive attitude. A new style of living needs to be found to match a new situation, which isn't worse than the paid work days, but is different. It could be one of the best periods of our lives, where we learn what it really means to be a useful person.

The Christian faith offers a radical alternative to a work-dominated culture. The Christian man will feel the stress of having no paid job like anyone else, but he can take hope from Christ's teaching.

Worth not work

The Christian man knows that God accepts him for who he is, and not for what he does. We are never useless to God, because he doesn't see us in terms of usefulness.

Tough times

We know that God is able to see us through the tough times, turning them to our advantage. We also know that he will go on loving, no matter how angry or frustrated we get. Nothing can separate us from his love.

Provision

We know that God will provide for our needs. Those without paid work face anxiety over money, bills and food. We know that God will not let us starve, and that he will meet our needs in many ways—gifts of food, cash and second-hand clothes.

Does it matter what other people think?

It's hard to watch other men going to work when we have to stay at home. What do those working men think of us? The media have told us that they think we are scroungers, malingerers, men who won't work because we prefer state benefit. The truth is that they probably don't think this about us at all. We seldom consider the sufferings of others, until these sufferings come to us. Men with paid work are glad to have it, and tend not to think about those without work.

It is hard to live in an environment where some work and some don't, and we can come under pressure by worrying about what others are thinking about us. This pressure can also affect our families. Our wives have to manage on less money that other women, and have to make do, while they see others getting new things. Our children have to go without, while they see their friends getting new clothes and plenty of money.

How can we live so that we are not for ever worrying about what others are thinking?

Not criminals

Having no paid work is not a crime, but a circumstance. It may pass, but if it doesn't then we have to learn to live with it. There are much more important things in life than worrying about what others think.

The simple life

Our consumer society wants us to have all the latest gadgets, and tries to convince us that we cannot live without them. But we can manage very well without a car, a continental holiday and a telephone. Many are finding that a simpler lifestyle, with less stress and less luxury is very fulfilling.

Approaching our circumstances like this is much more creative and positive. We are pioneering a new way of living, which might become the envy of our working friends. A change of attitude is required to think like this, and such changes are never easy. We've got to stop looking back to paid working days, and comparing them with the current situation, and start seeing the current situation as a new phase of our lives, with a new challenge and new hopes.

God is my reference point

On a personal note, I am answerable to God alone for what I am and what I do, and what he feels about me is what matters. So I've never been unduly concerned about what others are thinking about me. It isn't that I don't care about others, and I don't like it when they think badly of me, but it doesn't matter to me when they do. This is my way of coping with what others think of me, and I know it works.

How can I manage on less money?

When we lose our paid job, we usually have to manage on less money, and this is not easy. Bills still have to be paid, and the family supported, however hard we try to economize. It's not easy watching the adverts on TV, and knowing that most of those things are beyond our reach. How can we cope?

Become a hermit

In a desperate attempt to relieve the pressure everything gets cut to the bare minimum. There are no luxuries, treats or relaxations. This approach might have the desired effect, but it will destroy us as people. Relaxation and holiday are not luxuries, but an essential part of our creative lives.

Ignore the situation

This approach will work for a time, but only for a time. Eventually the money will run out, or the credit company will want repayment.

Act

This is the obvious and best approach. We need to take some action which will help us live within our budget, and yet still leave us some room to manoeuvre. It we act first, before the pressures get too great, then at least we will have some freedom of choice. If we leave it until everything is falling apart, then we will have to act as outside forces direct. Most men would prefer to have some freedom of choice.

So what action can we take, and how?

Be honest. Be honest about finances, especially with your wife. For far too long we've been too secretive about our earnings.

Keep it in perspective. Don't let financial matters get too prominent. They are necessary, but are only one part of life. A secure marriage, health and peace of mind are much more precious, and can't be given a price tag.

Balance the budget. We need to know what our fixed commitments are, so that we can set money aside for them. We also need to try and make some allowance for the extras that make life worth living. Have you ever sat down and done this, alone or with your wife? Fixed commitments like mortgage or credit have to be considered carefully. Falling behind with these can lead to serious trouble.

Forget credit. Credit cards are a real danger. Why not send them back, and use cash or cheques for purchases? Credit looks good but is very expensive. Be careful before committing yourself.

Remember free is beautiful. Seasides are free. Walks are free. Libraries are free. For relaxations, start to look for the many cheap or free enjoyments.

Take holidays nearer home. Don't abandon holiday—it's vital to us—but look nearer home for cheaper alternatives to the continent.

Seek help. There is help around for those who want guidance over their financial affairs, and have no paid work. Are you too proud to ask?

Personally I leave the budget to God. I am still expected to be a steward of what he gives me, and to account to him for it, but in the end, he has promised to provide the bread and butter of life, and occasionally cake as well. I don't find this too much of a problem. Like many other full-time Christian workers, Mary and I have lived this way for years.

What if I'm made redundant?

A friend of mine has been made redundant three times. On each occasion he has passed through the same series of experiences:

* At first, he just shrugs his shoulders, and accepts the situation. Everybody thinks that he will be fine.
* For a while everything *is* fine. He finds plenty to do at home.
* Then he starts to feel that life is pointless. His marriage begins to get tense. His wife does all she can to try and give him encouragement, and looks out for odd jobs he can do.
* Slowly, he comes to realize that he isn't going to get another job. This helps him begin to accept what has happened, and to look for new meaning in his life.

My friend's experience is typical of those who lose their jobs. A redundant man loses so many things—his income, his place in society, a purpose to life, regular contact with other men, his sense of worth and value, his manliness. Coming to terms with this loss is like coming to terms with the death of a loved one. It's long, slow and painful. It's made worse by seeing other men having work, and by living in a society that values paid work almost above life itself.

While it's not possible to hide the basic pain, there are some courses of action open to us:

Be honest and accept the hurt

One of our greatest weaknesses as men is our refusal to be honest about our feelings. We so quickly hide behind our tough-guy masks. But hurts that are hidden only hurt even more. Redundancy is a painful experience, and needs to be faced as such. If we are honest about these feelings, then we will be able to find a way forward.

Many men have survived the experience of redundancy. It is a dreadful experience, but not a terminal one. Life goes on, and can be a better experience if we will let it.

Look to new patterns

Our lives are of greater value than the money we receive through paid work. We are not worthless because we are not working.

We have got to find new ways of living which will suit our new circumstances. This is never an easy process, especially if we are not young. But new patterns can and will emerge if we're willing to make the experiment, and are prepared to give ourselves time. There's nothing wrong with taking time to think, evaluate and experiment. There is no need to hurry.

Look for help

Others have been this way before us, and there is help around, both in books and in self-help groups. Why do we struggle on alone, when others might be able to help us find a way ahead? Men don't find it easy to accept help, but there are times when it's just foolish to go on alone.

The Christian man knows that God doesn't evaluate worth by paid work. We are valuable to God as we are. We know that God can handle pain—even the pain of losing a paid job, and that he can turn it all to good, although sometimes we don't understand how he can do it. Most of all, we know that God's plan for our lives is always for now, not for yesterday. In paid work or out of it, we are in his plan. This gives us great confidence in times of bewilderment.

What if I'm ill?

Men face illness with much less reality than women. We are less likely to go to the doctor when we are ill and we find it harder to make adjustments because of chronic illness.

These facts alone mean that when we have to give up work through illness we are in for a tough time. But the hardest pressure for us is the pressure on our masculinity. To lose a job through illness is a tremendous challenge to our ego and pride. We feel that we are no longer real men because we can't hold down a job, or properly support our wife and family. It's a great humiliation for us, and the future can look very bleak. How can we possibly go on?

There are no neat and tidy answers here—there never are when paid work stops. But there are a few factors worth considering:

Opportunity

Physical illness gives us an opportunity to get to know ourselves in a very real way. It gives time for thought about values beyond work, pay and material things.

Alternatives are not good

Leaving work through physical illness feels really bad, but the alternative is to be carried by others, which isn't a very manly experience. Staying on can also lead to serious mistakes, and a rapid worsening of the illness.

Work is not worth

We are more valuable than the paid work we do. Our value as a person does not cease because illness forces us to leave paid work. We have a unique contribution to make, and it's possible that paid work has been stopping us from making that contribution.

Strength is not worth

There is much more to a man than physical strength, however desperate the loss of that strength may seem to us. Our masculinity does not depend on our strength, but on our character, and our way of living.

The Christian man has a very different perspective on serious physical illness. He brings all his hurt to a God that deals in eternity. We are all going to waste away ultimately, but the Christian man knows that he will not be wasted eternally. This gives strength for the present, and keeps present sufferings in some kind of perspective.

Strongly linked to this eternal perspective is the conviction that no one has ever been retired from, invalided out of, or made redundant in God's army.

How can I find a job?

Finding paid work is not always easy. The amount of openings varies in different places, and a lot depends on what skill we have to offer, and where we are offering it. There are many agencies offering help, and the man looking for paid work must make use of them. But even before he does, it's useful to face a few basic facts:

* Why do I want paid work? It's important to examine motives at the outset. Do we believe that paid work will improve us as people, or are we really unable to face the emptiness of life without paid work?
* Will paid work improve the quality of my life? Or am I trading many of the benefits of not having paid work for the money that paid work will bring?
* What have I got to offer? Be realistic. Many may be offering the same things, and they may have a lot of advantages.
* Am I willing to take a lower paid job?
* Am I willing to take a different job? It isn't always easy to change types of job. What will be the total effect of such a change on your life? It's like being a beginner again, even though thirty working years may have passed in one job or skill.
* Am I willing to move? This needs careful consideration. A move might bring paid work, but it also means a new home, living in a new area, new schools, new relationships. This is always a risky thing to do, especially if we are older. Starting again gets harder as the years pass. But there are also advantages in moving—new challenges and opportunities, new friends and new interests.

* What is available in my area? Every avenue needs to be explored, and every contact followed up.
* Can I retrain?
* Am I well prepared when opportunities come? Interviews have to be prepared for, and the casual approach could be disastrous.
* Do I give up too easily? It might take many interviews until things work out. Becoming depressed by constant rejection happens all too easily. Being with others who are in the same search is a great advantage. It's worth looking into the alternatives to paid work in your area and community. These openings can help us to feel useful, and to be useful while searching for paid work.

The Christian man faces the same issues, the same challenges, and the same long road of search. He also faces two extra questions:

* What does God want me to do?
* Is God using this circumstance to call me into his service in some way—full time, part time or to work in the community?

How can I start a new life?

When we brought our first child home from hospital fifteen years ago, everyone told us that we would experience changes in our way of life. At first, things stayed much the same. David lay in his pram, and it was lovely. But slowly he made his presence felt, and we had to change almost everything to accommodate him.

A man who has lost his paid job has to look for new patterns of life. These new patterns don't come immediately, but they must come, if we're going to have a good quality of life. But they must come slowly, as we adapt to a new situation. What can help the new ways to come?

Facing the need

When our first son arrived, it soon became obvious that we couldn't go out much in the evenings. We recognized this fact, and abandoned much of our evening social life. In much the same way, a man who has no paid work has to recognize the need to change, and to look for new patterns of life. Until we reach this point of acceptance, the new patterns will always be stifled.

Reassessment

Once we had faced the need to change with our first son, then we began to reassess all of our lives. The man with no paid work must do the same:

* What lifestyle am I leading?
* What might need to be changed?
* What sort of person am I?

* What changes can I make now that I couldn't make while
  I was working?

Reassessing our lives for David wasn't easy, but we
approached it in a positive way. We were moving into something different and better. This same positive approach is
vital for those with no paid work. Have you adopted the
positive approach?
    Finance also needs to be reassessed and put on a sound
footing. There may be commitments that have to be stopped
or lowered. Certain things that have always been seen as
necessities need to be examined carefully. Less expensive
ways of relaxing and fun need to be found. Getting this
matter right in a society that places such value on wealth and
possessions isn't going to be easy.

Ask yourself some questions:
Some questions need to be faced honestly about the past:

* Did I always enjoy my job?
* Were there other things that I wanted to do, but couldn't
  because of work?
* Can I manage on my new income?
* Are there opportunities ahead of me right now that I could
  take?

Learning from others

It might be helpful to look at how others have managed to
build a new life—both well-known figures and the couple
round the corner. These people might give us valuable tips,
and help us avoid trouble spots.

Working it out with the family

New patterns will have to be worked out with wife and
children. This is a very difficult area, because it means that
they will have to change their patterns as we change ours.
But this can also lead to a deeper marriage and a more secure
family life. We need to spend some time with our wife, talking
things over.

Those who follow Christ know all about new patterns of life. The last section of this book will give you some idea of just how new and different his way is.

Will my marriage stand the strain?

When a husband has a paid job, he spends much of his life separated from his wife. So each partner develops their own timetable and way of life. While the husband makes friendships at work, his wife has her own pattern at home, with her own circle of friends. She might even have a job of her own programmed in to her other responsibilities.

When the husband loses his paid job, he is at home all day. His timetable and pattern are broken, and his presence forces his wife to change her patterns. This produces many stress areas:

* He is depressed and aimless.
* Her life and pattern are disrupted, which unsettles her.
* The future looks uncertain, and causes worry to both partners.
* The children cause concern—there is the need to provide for them, but with limited means.
* The husband is not clear about his role in the marriage. It's worse if his wife works, leaving him alone all day.
* Priorities have to be sorted out, and cut backs planned for. This always causes tension.
* Old problems in the marriage re-emerge, and old doubts resurface.

Most married people face this kind of pressure when the man loses his paid job. It's so easy to think that we are the only ones going through it. But there is another side to this picture. More time together can mean a deeper and richer marriage, with more time for the children and for other people.

What steps might need to be considered in order to enjoy a richer marriage experience after losing paid work?

Willingness to work at it

Marriages need to be worked at if they are going to work. There needs to be time to talk, time to be together, time to relax, time with the children. We will never achieve richer marriages without a lot of effort and commitment. Are you prepared to make the effort?

Re-adjustment

Re-adjustments will be necessary at every level of the marriage. This is not going to be easy, especially as men are not good at sharing their feelings and thoughts. There will have to be a lot of give and take, and we should be willing to make the major sacrifices, for the sake of our wife and children. Are you willing that this should happen?

Being honest

It's easy to say that we will work at our marriage, but the personal cost will be high. Are you prepared to be open and honest about your feelings and attitudes? Are you prepared to be told that you are wrong, and accept it? Are you prepared to change?

Taking advice

It's good to have someone who is outside our marriage, with whom we can talk openly. This is not to be a substitute for talking to our wives, but sometimes we need a little extra encouragement from a sympathetic outsider.

Christian marriages face as great a strain as any, but the Christian man has some extra encouragements:

* He knows that his marriage is in the hand of God. This gives him confidence in his marriage, and courage in the face of marital strains.
* He knows that God wants the best for his marriage, and that if he is willing, God will let the best become a reality.

* He is still the head of his wife and family, whether he has paid work or not. This gives no licence for arrogance, or chauvenism, but it does help him to keep a sense of balance in an uncertain situation.

What if my wife needs to work?

When a man loses his paid work, the family income drops dramatically. In these circumstances, many wives feel that they should go out to work. Before this happens there are certain issues that every couple should face:

Need

Does the wife need to work, or is this just an excuse to continue to maintain a high standard of living?

Challenge

When the wife works, a man will naturally feel a threat to his masculinity, because being able to provide for our families is so central to us as men. We may have to learn to live with this challenge, but if it is so strong that it is upsetting the marriage, is the extra money gained worth it?

Strain

Sometimes a working wife can throw great strain on the marriage and family. Even though the husband might do all he can, he isn't a mother, and can't replace her. Is the strain worth the money?

Fulfilment

Sometimes work helps our wives to fulfil themselves as people. Are you willing to allow this to happen, for the benefit of the marriage?

Christians must bring this matter to God. What we are looking for is his best for our marriage and family. If the marriage and family are damaged by the wife working, then no amount of extra finance will make up for it, and we will have to answer to God for letting it continue. We profess to believe in his provision for us, and so we need the courage to see what this means in practical terms—whether it be our wife working, less expenditure, or more reliance on prayer. We need the full courage of our convictions.

SECTION SIX

Singleness

How can I live with singleness?

It's not easy being a single man in a society where most people are married. It's not so much a problem when we are young, because there are many single teenagers around, but the difficulties increase when we begin to move out of the teenage years. This isn't true for all single men. Some choose singleness, and enjoy it to the full. But those who would prefer to be married face physical, emotional and social frustrations. The fact that most married people have little or no idea of the pain of enforced singleness, and are even suspicious of it, doesn't make matters any easier.

How can a single man live with singleness, and still enjoy a creative life? I've written more on this subject in my book *The Christian Man* (Kingsway, 1986), but here are some of the areas he must consider:

There is a problem

Being single while wanting to be married presents certain problems which are best faced, rather than ignored:

* Some people will wonder if 'there's something wrong with you'.
* Opportunities for social life will be restricted. Married people tend to go out with married people.
* Loneliness is a constant pressure.
* Relationships with women will be awkward, and open to misunderstanding.

These problems might last for a long time. Facing them openly will be painful, but is much more realistic than hiding from them, or pretending that they don't matter.

It's not all bad news

Single men enjoy certain opportunities and privileges that a married man has surrendered. He has time to use as he wills, flexibility of employment, money to use, hobbies to follow up, community interests, and so on. These are not substitutes for female company and marriage, but they are there to be used and enjoyed. A single man who ignores them because he doesn't have a wife, will never get any fulfilment from life, and will probably look very dull and uninteresting to any woman.

You don't have to continue alone

A single man needs to share some of the pain of unwanted singleness with a friend. This keeps things in perspective, and stops him getting too isolated. It isn't going to be easy to share his feelings—men never find it so. But it is going to be a great help. Another single friend will understand best, but he may be too involved with singleness to be able to be objective. A married friend is out of the situation, so can probably be more detached, but on the other hand he doesn't really understand what you are going through. Against this background, choices have to be made.

A Christian single man feels the pain like any other. But he has the advantage of knowing that God is in control of his life. This doesn't take away the immediate pain, but it does put it in a wider perspective. He can live his life to the full now, knowing that God has a perfect plan for him, and that he's too big to make a mistake. If the current phase of the plan calls for singleness then he can move forward into that with confidence rather than for ever regretting that the plan doesn't call for marriage.

Ultimately a single man needs to be a fighter. He needs to decide on how he's going to tackle the problems, and then take them on one by one. If being married is an honourable estate, then so is being single. We need to take pride in it.

Who do I love?

I've just been visited by my youngest son. As I sat here, thinking what to write, he pushed open the door, climbed over my papers, sat on my knee, kissed me while his mouth was full of chocolate, and then left, leaving me to clean up! I wouldn't exchange that moment for anything. To be loved by another human being, even if he is covered in chocolate, is a precious experience.

We all need love, however grown up we may be. To give it and receive it makes us truly satisfied, and to be without it is a great loss. Men are not in the habit of talking about love, but they need to both give and receive it from women and men. The world's attitudes have made this process difficult for us, branding male love as homosexual and female love as flirtatious. But, as usual, the world is wrong.

Single men are in a very vulnerable position. Living alone, they can lose the art of loving, and when they do try to give love, it can be misunderstood.

We all need love

Single men are no different from anyone else—we all need to give and receive love. It's crucial that single men do not lose sight of this truth. It is a difficult area, and there are many opportunities for mistakes and hurt. But it's vital not to give up because of the mistakes. Once the art of loving is lost, a real hardness can come, which is very difficult to overcome.

Ways of showing it

The only way to retain the art of loving is to find ways of showing affection for men and women which are not open to misunderstanding. For example:

* Doing practical things with other people, and enjoying being together on these tasks.
* Giving time to everyone in a group, and not just to the ones we like.
* Taking care who we cuddle!
* Taking every opportunity to talk and be with people, especially in the twelve to thirty-five age range. This is the area where most misunderstandings can occur, but if we don't take opportunities to talk and be with them, we'll forget how to be with them.

A Christian man has a great advantage in that he belongs to a church family. In this family we will find:

* There are women we can talk to, with less risk of mis-understanding.
* In the small groups that most churches have, sharing of personal needs is encouraged. This helps us to be honest about our needs.
* In the church, we can learn to love the unlovable.
* In the family of God, we are constantly reminded that we are loved by Christ with a love that will never end, no matter what we are, or what we do.

How do I use my time?

We all have 168 hours a week to use in whatever way seems right to us. Married men and single men will obviously make different use of their time, because of their different commitments. A single man has the difficulty of living with loneliness. When he gets home from work, the things he left in the morning are in exactly the same place. There's no one to share his day with, and however much he tries to interest himself, the walls of his room can soon begin to close in. A married man has a wife to talk to, and can always just relax back into the family routine.

How can a single man live with the time he has, and make creative use of it?

Face the truth

Time can be a problem for single men. Facing this truth is hard, but it is realistic, and realism is the key to so many of the issues that face us. Some days are going to be worse than others, and time will hang very heavy. These days—and they can come to married as well as single men—just have to be endured. Tomorrow is always another day.

Think positive

Time is a precious commodity. There is much that can be done with it, if we are prepared to think in a creative and positive way. For example:

* Time can be used creatively—to make, do, learn, travel.
* Time can be used to develop and maintain friendships, to help others and to serve the community.

Is there an escape from loneliness?

We all feel lonely from time to time, but it's a greater pressure on a single man, because he has more time to be alone than a married man.

Face it honestly

There will be times, perhaps extended times, when we are going to be lonely. This fact needs to be faced.

Learn through it

Loneliness, or solitude, gives us a chance for reflection, quiet and personal growth. So much of our Western culture denies this basic need, but it is there and needs to be fulfilled.

Watch it

It's vital that we don't let periods of solitude get so long or intense that we lose touch with the world. This is where we need our friendships, which need to be natural and easy going, built for the joy they give to each, and not just as an escape from loneliness.

The Christian single man can gain much encouragement from Christ, who was single himself, and often alone. Within the family of the church, there are also many opportunities to meet and mix with others, as a balance to times of solitude.

How do I get female company?

Recently, I toured England speaking to groups of men. When I got home, I had obviously lost some of my gentleness and sensitivity towards Mary, because she remarked, 'I can tell that you've been spending most of your time with men!'

Men need female company—it helps us keep a balance in our behaviour, our outlook and our attitudes. Married men get this company easily—from their wives and from other women. But it's not so easy for single men. There's no wife to mix with, and relationships with women in general are not always easy or natural. In the background, there's always the question of motive. Yet as one single man commented: 'There's nothing quite so therapeutic as spending time with girls that you find attractive in every sense.'

How can a single man go about enjoying female company in this therapeutic way, while at the same time avoiding the misunderstandings that can so easily arise?

Face facts

This is a difficult and delicate area, where mistakes and embarrassments abound.

Look for opportunities

We need to look for opportunities where we can enjoy female company in non-threatening circumstances. We can do this in interest or hobby groups, or we could invite a group of friends round from work for an evening, or lunch. We mustn't give up the desire to enjoy female company, because the fullness of our human nature needs this experience. Even if we make mistakes, and are hurt, this shouldn't deter us from trying again.

Watch our motivation

We need to keep a careful check on our motives. Women are very generous in their actions, so it's up to us to be very clear about our motives, and scrupulous in our behaviour. It's very easy for us to let things get out of hand, or to read more into a relationship than is there. Some friendships will develop and lead to marriage. But if we begin to doubt our motives in others, it's probably better to break the relationship, if only for a while.

How do I cope with sex and stay human?

Our sexual emotions and feelings are an important part of us, and they are wholly good. It's very important to recognize this fact, as we try to work out our approach to sex and our sexual feelings. Problems come to us for a number of reasons:

* Society has spoilt and warped these emotions, and as a consequence, many of us think and do evil things.
* Television, newspapers and advertising play on our sexual emotions in a distorted way.
* The way women dress and behave often arouses us, and leads us to misunderstand their motives and intentions.

These sexual pressures come to all of us—married or single—but are far harder to resolve for the single man. How can a single man live with his sexual feelings, in such a way that he remains a normal male?

Accept that they're not wrong

It's not wrong to have sexual emotions and feelings. It's vital for single men to realize this, because they have no wife nearby to help them in this understanding.

Try to talk to someone

It's so easy to make mistakes in this area of our lives, and to get confused, embarrassed or hurt. It's not always easy to know what course of action is right. It's not always easy to get outside help, because we get embarrassed about our sexual feelings.

Try to understand the male/female difference

Men and women are very different in sexual matters. Men are much more physical—we like to touch and see. We keep our lives in compartments, so that what happens at work won't affect how we feel sexually. Women are more concerned with personality, with surroundings, and can't separate their sexual lives from the rest of their daily lives.

If we do not understand this and other differences, we will so easily misunderstand gestures and comments. It's so easy to think we're being led on by a woman, when in fact we're wrongly interpreting her gestures, because we're understanding them from a masculine point of view.

Learn control

It's essential that we control our eyes and our thoughts. If we let them run away with us, we're going to get hurt, and hurt others. This is a very tough course of action, but it's one of the keys to remaining a friendly and approachable man.

We can aid the control process by having ways of changing our thoughts and behaviour when they threaten to get out of control. We may find that we can put extra energy into work or sport, take a shower, go for a walk—anything to break a pattern of thought.

Avoid triggering situations

Another element of control is to stay away from situations that trigger wrong sexual feelings. This might include some newspapers and books, some TV films and certain people and events. We need to face our feelings, and have the courage to walk away, or not even to go.

Christian men face the same challenge. The only difference is that we have an extra dimension in our faith in God, who works within us, doing for us what we cannot do for ourselves. We also have the means of forgiveness when we fail, and we will need that many times. We don't have to feel condemned by our failures.

Why can't I just sleep around?

There's nothing to stop a single man sleeping around if he feels like it. In fact he can even save himself the trouble of looking for a woman if he goes to the right place and pays the right price.

Why should men want to sleep around in the first place?

* They have a very high opinion of themselves and their needs.
* They have no control over themselves.
* They place a very low value on women and their needs and expectations.

Many men don't go this far, but that doesn't make them saints. For some, it's just that they have lacked the opportunity or the nerve. Part of the pressure to sleep around comes from a low moral standard in society, that sees this as a harmless 'adult' practice. There are also men around who boast of their exploits, and consequently make other men feel that if they're not sleeping around, they are not real men.

The man who doesn't want to follow this path might feel that he is swimming against the tide, but he has much to encourage him:

Health guaranteed

He can be sure that he will not contract venereal disease or AIDS.

Right with God

He can be sure that he is in the right with God, for God expressly forbids this kind of behaviour, seeing it as no less than rape.

Right regard for women

Women are not objects to be used to gratify our uncontrolled sexual desires. They are people, and their bodies are for their husbands alone to enjoy. The man who refuses to sleep around is recognizing this as the truth.

In control

The man who doesn't sleep around is a man in some control of himself, which is a good and manly attribute. The man who gives in to sexual pressure is the weak man, no matter how good his story sounds in the bar, club or office.

This is not an easy temptation to resist, whether it be in fact or in our fantasies, but we do not need to succumb to it. We only give in, and lose the fight, if we choose to.

Why can't I get married?

There are many good reasons why a man cannot get married, and it's good to know this, because we can so easily think the fault is all ours. For example:

* The opportunity might not have presented itself.
* The right woman might not have come along.
* The right woman might have come, and we didn't ask her!
* We are looking for 'Miss Perfect', and she's proving hard to find.
* We're too shy to approach a girl.
* We've been hurt by previous encounters, and so, to prevent ourselves being hurt again, we won't make any approaches.
* We've lost the ability to communicate with women.
* We're too scared about making a mistake.
* We don't believe that any woman would be interested in us.

How does a single man live with the situation, even though he hopes that it might change in the future?

We are valuable

We don't have to be married to have worth and purpose. We are valuable as we are, no matter how much we think that marriage might increase our worth and give purpose to our lives.

We are not alone

It's easy to feel isolated because we can't get married. But there are many other people in the same state—it's just that we seldom talk about these very personal things. It would be good to have someone who would share our isolation. Do you have such a friend, and are you prepared to be honest with him?

Romance is a mystery

Being men, we like to be able to explain things. But romance cannot be explained in rational terms. What makes for mutual attraction and lasting relationships is indefinable. It isn't necessarily our fault that we didn't make a relationship with a particular girl—it has to be accepted as a mystery.

Check up

It's worth asking a good friend if he can see any reasons why we are having problems. There might be some obvious faults, which can be easily rectified—bad breath, manners, behaviour.

Learn to relax

If we are going to form relationships that lead to marriage, then we have to be ourselves with girls. After all, this is the person they will be marrying. It's so easy to put on a front to try and impress—but this has to be resisted. The irony is that our fronts probably make us less attractive to women.

Am I unattractive to women?

A man that wants to get married but can't is bound to come up against this question. It raises some very painful issues, which need to be faced:

Bad habits

Do I have any personal habits, or do I behave in a way that might put women off me? Try asking a close friend about this.

Wrong message

Sometimes we act in such a way that women who might be interested assume that we're not interested in them. This can happen because we're nervous, or because we are desperate to impress. We need to learn to be natural, and to show interest as far as we can, without going too far.

Courting

We're often in such a hurry, but women need to be courted. There's a lot to this approach—tenderness, gentleness, patience and understanding, gifts, treats, visits, time and good manners. This all takes time, and time is needed, as each make deeper steps of commitment. We also need to remember that different women appreciate a different approach. We need to be flexible and sensitive.

Confidence

We need confidence in ourselves as people. So often single men devalue themselves, believing that no one would be interested in them. But we are all attractive in some way, and if the woman we are courting doesn't like us, it isn't necessarily a personal rebuff—it's just part of the mystery of love.

Nothing is impossible

As a minister, I've married many couples of every age and type. I've learnt that the most unlikely couples get together and make their marriages work. Love is a mystery, and within it nothing is impossible.

Those of us who are committed to Christ know that we are uniquely precious and special to him—married or single. However unattractive we feel, we know that we are always beautiful to him. He helps heal the wounds of loneliness, or of failed relationships, as well as helping in our relationships with all people. If marriage is not his plan for you, he will help you through disappointment, to a deeper experience of him. If it is, he will lead you eventually to the right woman. We have to have a rugged confidence in his plan.

What if I feel attracted to other men?

We all need to give and receive love, from men and from women. This need must be met, if we are to be truly human. The world sees problems in men giving and receiving love from other men, quickly branding such relationships as homosexual. The world needs to be ignored on this as on so many other issues. Jesus Christ was not afraid to give and receive love from men, recognizing its necessity, and this gives us a very strong base from which to affirm our need of love from other men.

There is a danger, however, in male relationships. It is that we trespass beyond the bounds of love, into infatuation and sexual behaviour. God is quite clear that this is a state of affairs which he will not condone. It is a distortion of his creation and his will.

Quite a large percentage of men have homosexual tendencies, while not quite such a large percentage practise homosexuality. Society has done little to help such men, except to treat them with contempt, to pass draconian laws against them, and to leave them to be abused and ill treated.

If you think that you have a homosexual problem, it's worth knowing that God is loving, can forgive any sin, and build a new life for you. There are also some people around who can help. You might like to try: True Freedom Trust, PO Box 3, Upton, Wirral, Merseyside.

There is also a helpline for Christian parents of homosexuals: tel. 01 499 5949.

What about masturbation and erotic thoughts?

All of us face the pressures that these two problems bring. We all like looking at women, and this can so easily lead to erotic thoughts and fantasies. Sexual release can be found in a limited way through masturbation, but it brings us guilt and shame. How can we approach these two problems?

We're not alone

All of us have to face these issues at some time in our life. It's not an excuse, but it's an encouragement to know that we are not alone.

It's worth the fight

It's so easy to give in to these pressures—many do. But it's worth the fight to resist them, because both are demeaning experiences.

Look away

Women are beautiful, but they have not been created to be objects of our lustful thoughts. They are people in their own right. We must resist the thoughts, and avoid the situations, that give opportunity for them. We have to develop the habit of looking away, and of controlling our minds.

Re-direct energy

Masturbation is a mechanical process, and as such it is not wrong. But the thoughts that go with it are wrong, and do nothing to build us up as people. When it is over, we feel guilty and ashamed. Habits are hard to give up, but we need to find ways of breaking the habit—by doing other things, or directing our energies into other sources. We must also avoid situations, books and TV that we find unhelpful.

A lot of guilt can accompany these two pressures, but God can deal with guilt. It's hard for us to realize sometimes how much he longs to forgive us, to clean us up, and to help us start again.

Are you in need of his forgiveness today?

SECTION SEVEN

God

Is there a God?

Many men are genuinely interested in this question, and have an opinion to share. Many of these opinions, however, are not based on serious thought, but on what others have said or done.

I started to believe in God when I was very young. When I grew older, I tested my belief against what I could see and think. I wanted my faith to be based on what I thought, not on what others had told me. Here are some of the facts which helped me, and I believe they will help any man who genuinely wants to know more about God.

Creation

Some people think that creation can be explained by scientific fact. But the majesty and the mystery of creation defy total factual explanation. No one can factually explain the feelings we get in the middle of a great forest, on a mountain, or beside a stormy sea. The Bible tells us that through these feelings we are sensing something of the personality of God. To dismiss these experiences as mere feelings is foolish, for our feelings are as important to our understanding of our existence as are facts.

Conscience

Countries make laws, but it isn't laws that help us know right from wrong. Each of us has an inner objective standard, which we call our conscience. We can suppress it, ignore it or override it, but we cannot erase it. Some say that our conscience is the result of centuries of conditioning. But Christians believe that it is a reflection of God's objective standards.

The Bible

The Bible claims that there is a God, and that he can be known by us and wants a special relationship with us. Many people dismiss the Bible, but they do so without ever having read what it says. Such people don't want to be disturbed in their prejudices! Only a fool would dismiss the world's greatest book without having made some attempt to understand its message.

I wasn't trained at college to believe in the Bible. I came to it by chance, or so it seemed. As I read with an open mind, I was impressed with its honest appraisal of human nature, its realism and its relevance to me. It told of a God who loved and cared for people like me; a God who did not want to stand outside of my life, judging how well I managed, but who wanted to be involved with me, helping to bring meaning and colour to my experience.

It is not possible to positively prove the existence of God. Indeed God himself always refused to provide such proof, believing that it would force belief, which he doesn't want. But the combined evidence of creation, conscience and the Bible provides a strong base from which further searching can take place with confidence.

Why should I believe?

Men have been brought up to believe that they are masters of their own destinies. This feeling of control is tied up with our view of masculinity. We feel that it's good and manly to be in control of the situations in which we are involved.

Men with this attitude tend to reject God, fearing that to believe in him will mean surrendering control and therefore some of their masculinity. The price of belief seems very high, and they decide to stay as they are.

God does want us to know him, and in order to do so we must surrender control of our lives to him. But in return for our willing surrender, he offers many benefits.

Friendship

The believing man has exchanged loneliness for a personal friendship with a loving and caring God. For God is not a cloud, but a person. He speaks, thinks, makes decisions, and wants to communicate with us.

Manliness

Worldly men are looking for ways to be real men. The tough-guy image is an attempt to fill this need, and it has been a disaster for masculinity. But the man who believes in God knows that he will achieve his full potential. God will make real men of us, drawing on our strengths, and using us through our weaknesses. Men often say that being a Christian is soft, and not the sort of thing that real men need. But it takes great courage to follow Christ—the soft ones are the men who can't face a hard challenge. Facing the challenge ultimately brings great fulfilment—there is no more exciting and satisfying experience in the world than being a man in Christ's service.

Meaning

We all have to face suffering and pain in life. The man who wants control of his own life must struggle through as best he can, hoping that his luck will change, or that everything will turn out all right. The man who has given control to God knows that God will make sense of it all, will give strength to bear the pain, and will make us better men because of it.

Forgiveness

We all make mistakes. The unbelieving man, in control of his own destiny, has no way of getting rid of the guilt. The believing man brings all his mistakes to God, and knows both the joy of forgiveness and the privilege of making a fresh start each time. The believing man is delivered from the crippling effects of failure, because Christ is always able to forgive and help put things right. The unbelieving man must learn to live with his failures unaided.

Reassurance

The believing man has nothing to fear in death. He knows that God who has loved and cared for him in this life has power over death and will not abandon him in the next life. He knows where he is going, and he knows that God will look after the loved ones he leaves behind. In the face of death, men in control of their own destinies have a lot to worry about. The believing man only has a lot to look forward to.

How can I believe in a God of love when there's so much suffering around?

The question of suffering has always been a barrier to belief.

Some men use it as a smokescreen, to avoid the necessity of facing facts.

Some are genuinely perplexed by the contradiction between a God who is supposed to be a God of love, and the sufferings of the world.

Some have suffered themselves, and so feel acutely hurt by a God of love who didn't help them when they called on him.

Some suffering in the world is due to our own foolishness. If a man smokes heavily, he knows the risks he is running, and he must face the consequences.

But much suffering doesn't seem to be directly our fault, and is very perplexing. We faced this question in a very acute way when our son Philip died after only a few hours of life. We believed in God, we had prayed much, and so had many others. We had done all we could, and yet despite all the medical care, our baby died. The pain of that moment, and of the years that followed, was very hard to bear. How could our God let this happen to us? I was very angry with God, and it took me many years to fully regain my faith.

This is the kind of suffering which challenges belief. Why did Philip die? Why do so many starve? Why do earthquakes kill? The question of suffering has endless forms. But as those who have suffered will testify, suffering challenges us very deeply about our belief, or lack of it. The Bible tells us that God loves and cares about his creation. Part of the challenge of belief is to go on believing this in the face of apparently pointless suffering. Our response to this challenge will either turn us towards God, or away from him.

It's impossible to answer the question of suffering in a few pages. But suffering does not necessarily force us to deny the existence of God, and I feel that I have earned the right to ask you to give this some serious thought. Through our suffering Mary and I found our faith was stretched to the limits, but at the same time we never lost the sense of his presence, his compassion and his understanding.

Do I need God anyway?

Why should a man need God? Here are the answers of three men:

'It all depends what you're looking for. I wanted truth, and I only found it in God.' (A successful business man.)

'I went to a small meeting with my wife at the house of some Christian friends. As I listened to them talking about their faith, I realized that these people had something that I didn't have. I said to myself, 'OK, I can stay as I am, or I can see if I can find what they have found.' That night I started to learn about God, and it wasn't long before I found him for myself. I wouldn't be without him now for anything.' (A redundant man.)

'This is God's world. You can't live in God's world without God. Human nature was never designed to do it. You will bend and bend, until one day you will break.' (An experienced evangelist.)

Why does a man need God?

* Only God can forgive him for his sins, and set him free from guilt.
* Only with God can a man become truly a man, living in God's world without fear.
* Only God can offer a man the challenge that we all long for—the challenge to struggle, to fight, to suffer and to endure for a cause that really matters.
* Only God can help a man be truly a husband to his wife, and a father to his children.
* Only God can lead a man through the confusions of life with a sure hand.

* Only God can give a man truth.
* Only God can guarantee a man life in this life and life in the world to come.
* Only God can make a man feel that he matters in a world that tells him he doesn't.
* Only God can give a man power to change himself and the world.
* Only God can release a man from fear.
* Only God has any solution to the question of suffering.

If you are looking for a complete human experience, you will have to get to know God. Without him, life can never have any lasting meaning or value.

Have you the courage to shake off prejudices that you have inherited from other men, take an honest look at what others believe and make an honest search yourself?

What's God got to say to a man like me?

It's sometimes hard for men to accept that God has anything to say to them. This happens for a number of reasons:

* A man feels that he is in charge of his own life, and has no need of any outside help.
* A man is afraid of what God might say, and so refuses to listen.
* A man knows that the quality of his life is poor, and senses that a holy God might be offended, so he assumes that God would not want to speak to him anyway.

God has something to say to every man, whatever his condition. He has made it quite clear that he wants all men to come to know the truth—about him, about themselves, and about the world in which we live. What might he say to you?

You fool

Many men try to run their own affairs without reference to God. Such men are ignoring their own spiritual needs, and are putting all their trust in physical things—what they can do, what they can enjoy and what they can own. Jesus told a story about a man who did just this—who ignored God and put all his trust in his physical possessions. The story ends: 'God said to him, "You fool! This very night you will have to give up your life; then who will get all these things you have kept for yourself?"' (Luke 12:20).

Are you being a fool? Are you ignoring the spiritual facts of life? Are you putting all your trust in what you can see and own? Maybe the time has come for you to do some more serious thinking about God and about yourself.

Don't be afraid

Some men are just afraid of God, perhaps because of the half truths they have heard at school, or on their occasional visits to church. They fear that they will be overwhelmed by such a powerful person, and hesitate to get close to him. The ordinary shepherds, who were told about the birth of Jesus by an angel felt much the same, but the angel's first words to them give us a glimpse of God's heart: 'Don't be afraid!' (Luke 2:10).

The man who honestly wants to know about God need not be afraid. God loves us and wants us to know him.

You're wanted

My two youngest children get very dirty, and each night we bath them so that they can go to bed clean. We don't clean them up first and then put them in the bath. We put them in the bath dirty, and they come out clean.

This is God's message to every man. He wants to clean us up, and to make us his men, ready to serve him and to know the joy of being fully man here on earth.

The things in your life of which you are ashamed are not a barrier to knowing God. When we recognize the wrongs, we are beginning to understand the things of God, especially the greatness of his forgiving love.

What difference will he make?

When a friend of mine gave control of his life to Jesus Christ for the first time, he asked me what difference it would make to him. I told him that we would have to wait and see. After two weeks, he could see no difference, but his wife could. She said, 'You're not shouting at the children like you used to!'

When we get our lives right with God, many changes come over us, although most of them are gradual ones. Here are some of the changes that men have told me about—and any one of them could happen to you:

* For the first time in my life, I felt that I belonged to someone, and that what I did really mattered to God.
* I found such a relief—I knew that I was forgiven. A great weight fell from my shoulders.
* I began to see my prayers being answered. This was amazing—God listening to me and answering. This gave me confidence to pray more, and to ask for bigger and bigger things.
* I felt a real man. I didn't need to pretend any more, or try to look big. I was God's man, and you can't get any bigger than that!
* I began to take the leadership of my home seriously. It wasn't easy at first, but gradually my wife began to realize that I really wanted to help and encourage her.
* There were many changes in the way I behaved. They weren't all easy to accept, and my friends were a bit puzzled. But each change made me feel better in myself and closer to God. I suspect that there are more changes to come, but I can see that as a result of them, I'm more able to enjoy life.

* It's great to have a true friend in God. I had always wanted friends, but many of them weren't reliable. I've found one now that I know will never let me down.
* Losing a baby is a miserable experience. I don't understand why it happened, but I received great strength from God. I couldn't have managed without him.
* It's tough following Christ. He has such high standards and expects so much of me. Sometimes I feel that I just can't go any further. But the challenge to follow is so satisfying.
* The thing about God is that he deals in eternal dimensions. He's helped me see things as broader than just my physical life. I don't need to worry about death. I am not too keen about dying, because that can be very painful, but I've no fears beyond the grave.
* I've been amazed at what I've been able to do. When I first gave control of my life to God, I wasn't quite sure what would happen. I joined a small group where I learnt more about God. Within two years I was leading it myself! God has given me the strength and power to do things that I would never have imagined possible. I wonder what he's got in store for me next.
* I wondered what my friends at work would feel about my commitment to God. They had a go at first, but now it doesn't matter to me what they say. I only wish they could share my faith. It's good having a faith at work—it gives me a set of standards and a way to behave.

No one can tell you what God will do for you if you give control of your life to him. But he does make a difference, and millions of men can share that the difference is worth experiencing.

How do I start a friendship with God?

I have always known God from a very early age. My infant faith has just grown steadily over the years. There have been key moments over those years when I have made steps forward, but I can't point to a time or a place and say, 'That's when my faith started.'

My wife Mary went to church when she was young, and would have said that she did have a friendship with God. When she was twenty-three we went away on a Christian holiday. At a meeting one night, the speaker read these words from the Bible: 'Saul, Saul, why do you persecute me?' But Mary heard: 'Mary, Mary, why do you persecute me?' She realized that she had never given control of her life to Christ, and prayed then and there that he would take control. She can clearly point to the moment when her faith started.

Your faith might begin at a particular moment, or grow over many years. But if you genuinely want to know God, these are the steps you need to consider:

Start to search for yourself

There are a number of ways in which we can find out about God. Some have started their journey by reading a book about the Christian faith, or a biography of a Christian person. Why not have a look in your library or in a Christian bookshop? Most churches have a bookstall, and more and more have books which can be borrowed. Many have found God for themselves by reading the Bible. One prisoner had nothing to read in his cell, except the Bible. He read it, just to pass the time, and finished up by giving control of his life to God. It's worth reading a modern translation of the Bible, and there are many to choose from these days.

Some start going to church as a way of beginning the search. If one church seems unattractive, there are always others to visit.

Some go to listen to a Christian speaker, so that they can get some facts on which to make a decision.

When we begin to search for God, we assume that we're the ones who are making the effort. In fact, God is also looking for us, because he really wants to meet us. Jesus told us: 'The Son of Man came to seek and to save the lost' (Luke 19:10). You are not searching alone—God is involved in your search, and this has been a great encouragement to many men.

Be honest

As we search, we have to take an honest look at ourselves, and face this question, 'Am I good enough for God?' The closer we get to God the more conscious we become of our faults and failings. Until a man is honest about himself, he will never be able to find God.

Learn about Jesus

We can only get our lives right with God if we get to know Jesus Christ first. Why not:

* Get a book or video about him from a Christian bookshop.
* Ask a Christian friend to tell you about him.
* Read about him for yourself in Mark's Gospel (second book in the New Testament section of the Bible).

Jesus' death was very tough. (Read about it for yourself in Mark's Gospel chapters 14 and 15.) This was a manly way to die and he did it to deal with your sin—the very thing which separates you from God.

Surrender

A friendship with God is guaranteed when you give control of your life to Jesus Christ. He died on the cross to take away your sin, and came to life again to prove that he really had done it. Are you willing to surrender to him? You need to:

* Recognize that in his sight you are a wrong-doer.
* Believe that Jesus is the Son of God.
* Believe that Jesus died on the cross for you.
* Believe that Jesus came alive again from death, and wants you as one of his followers.

If you are willing to surrender on these terms, then here is a simple prayer that you might like to use.

> 'God, I'm truly sorry for the past.
>   I turn away from it, and I turn to you. Thank you that your Son died on the cross for me.
>   Please forgive me. I surrender my life to you. Come in and take control right now.
>   Give me your Holy Spirit, and make me more like Jesus.
>   I thank you.'

Ask God to show you what you should do next.

How do I know it's true?

Seventeen years ago, Mary and I got married. After a week of our honeymoon, my life seemed very much the same as it had before, except that I didn't have to take my girlfriend home each night! But as the weeks and months went by, I had to make more and more changes, and Mary did as well, as our lives began to merge together. After seventeen years, I can see what a great commitment I made on my wedding day.

When a man gives control of his life to Jesus Christ, he has made a very great commitment—as radical as marriage, and much longer lasting. How can he be sure that the faith he is believing in is true?

Sometimes, Christian men can think that it's wrong to ask this sort of question, and they feel guilty. But it's a vital question, it needs asking, and Christ has left us an indellible answer.

Three times before he died, he made this promise in public to his followers:

> We are going up to Jerusalem where the Son of Man [Jesus] will be handed over to the chief priests and the teachers of the Law. They will condemn him to death and then hand him over to the Gentiles, who will mock him, spit on him, whip him, and kill him; but three days later he will rise to life (Mark 10:33–34).

Because this promise was made in public, everyone would know that he was a liar if he didn't keep it. But three days after his death, he was seen alive again, first by a woman, then by his closest followers on a number of occasions, and on one occasion by over 500 people at once.

Jesus kept his promise to come alive again, and because he kept this promise, we can safely trust him for *all* his promises.

To encourage us in believing this promise, here are some further things to consider:

* The authorities wanted to prove that Jesus was a liar. All they had to do was to produce his body. They never did.
* Something happened to change eleven defeated men into world-changing men.
* The main churches have always taught that Jesus rose from the dead.
* Over a thousand million people believe that he did.

You can trust Jesus.

Will I feel out of place?

When we start believing in Jesus, many changes come to our lives. They don't all come at once, but they do come. We have different standards from those we live and work with, and our morals, our marriage, our family, our personal and spiritual lives all undergo major changes. We have different expectations, and we believe in prayer, the Bible, worship and service of others. (I've written extensively about all of these areas in *The Christian Man* [Kingsway, 1986].)

We will certainly feel different, but does this mean we feel out of place?

We are, in fact, very much in place. We are right with God, through our trust in Jesus. We are in line with God's plan and purpose for us, and are playing the right part in his world. We are in our right place—those who are not right with God are the ones who are out of place.

Friction

There will be a certain amount of tension between us and those who do not believe in God. As they are in the majority, we are bound to feel out of place. Some of them will certainly make our life difficult—by ridiculing us, insulting us and by ignoring us. But we must remember:

* It is not we who have the problem, even though we are a minority. We are right with God.
* Jesus faced the same problem. We must see it as a privilege to have the same experience as him.
* Men respect men of conviction, even if they can't share those convictions. As we endure the tension, we will gain credibility in the eyes of some who might begin to consider where they stand with God.

Does it really matter?

Does it really matter that we feel out of place? A friend of mine gave control of her life to Christ when she was at school. Her friends ridiculed her faith, but far from weakening her, it made her stronger. She said, 'I decided that as I was going to be laughed at for following Christ, I might as well follow him one hundred per cent. I left them to think and do what they liked.'

Let others think what they want. We must live for Christ.

What will my friends think?

If we are sensitive to the feelings of others, and most of us are, then we are going to wonder what others are going to make of our faith and our new ways of behaving. What will our friends say at work, or in the pub or club? If they start mocking us, we are going to feel very vulnerable and defenceless.

From my experience of this situation, friends can have a variety of reactions:

* *Disinterest.* They couldn't really care less.
* *Ridicule.* This soon becomes boring to them and they give up.
* *Admiration.* They don't believe themselves, but appreciate a man who makes a stand for what he believes.
* *Close observation.* They wait to see how things work out. Some will quickly spot a mistake, saying 'Is that the way Christians behave?'
* *Interest.* They are waiting to see what happens, because there is some stirring interest in their heart.
* *Apprehension.* Are we going to start carrying a Bible and singing hymns during our work break? Are we going to start moralizing, and reporting all their fiddles and faults? Are we going to stop being fun and start being boring?

We have to live with whatever reaction comes. The answer for us is to:

Continue to be ourselves

We shouldn't act as we think we should, or as we've seen others behaving. We must continue to be ourselves.

Let God lead

If there are changes to come, we must let God show us where
and when to make them. We're so often too keen to run ahead
of God. Let him lead and at his speed.

Take advice

Others have had the same problem. Meeting regularly with
other Christian men can help us through this period of our
lives. We don't have to be alone.

Keep smiling

We must not take all the comments thrown at us too seriously.
How would we have reacted if one of our friends had done
what we have done? Humour can help us, and it can help our
friends through this period.

As we explain what has happened to us, and why our
behaviour has changed, opportunities will come to help our
friends find their way to God.

In the end, our friends must think what they want to think.
We can only live for Christ, and let them make their own
decisions. In many cases reactions are much more favourable
than we might expect.

What will my wife and family think?

When a friend of mine gave his life to Christ, his wife said, 'I was utterly amazed!'

Wives usually are amazed when their husbands give control of their lives to Jesus Christ. They are usually delighted, occasionally angry, and often wondering what changes will come in the marriage, and in the family.

It's up to us to be loving and caring in a new way towards them. This helps wife and family realize that what has happened is going to result in a better marriage and home life.

My wife

It seems that generally women have a clearer understanding of spiritual things than do men. The result of this is that many wives have had to take the lead in spiritual matters. As we now take the lead spiritually, we need to be careful. It will take a wife some time to get used to our interest and concern. She will also need time to understand the changes in our life, which will affect the marriage. It's very important that husband and wife talk about the changes and learn to absorb them slowly.

My children

Children can also be concerned at what to expect. Will you want to sing hymns all the time? Are all books banned except the Bible? Is the fun going to go out of life? We need to take things easily with them, letting God take the lead. If we pray regularly about this, then slowly the children will respond to the greater love and security in the home.

My relatives

Our relatives may find our new lifestyle difficult to accept. They may find it hard to forget the old person that we were, and not make much allowance for our new faith. It's an area that needs prayer and patience.

The key in dealing with family and friends is time. They need time to think about what's happening and time to absorb the changes. They won't always understand, and need time to go away and think. They also have the right to reject faith in God, even though we believe strongly. But through time, and our prayers, we may have the chance to see many of them coming to know God for themselves.

How can I keep it up?

I clearly remember one man coming up to me after a meeting where I had spoken about faith in Christ and saying, 'Jim, I'll never keep it up.' I paused for a moment, and then replied, 'Good. Then you'll just have to trust God to keep it up for you.'

He was right in one way—we can never hope to keep our commitment. However hard we try, we will find that it's just too hard. God knows this, and so he's made provision to keep it up for us, and that provision is known as the Holy Spirit.

There are many books about the Holy Spirit, but the very best is what God says about him in the Bible. In the Acts of the Apostles (fifth book in the New Testament section of the Bible) it's possible to see the Holy Spirit at work. As we read this book, these facts will help us understand a little more clearly about how the Holy Spirit works:

* The Holy Spirit is the third person that makes up our God. (We know God as Father, Son and Holy Spirit.)
* The Holy Spirit is a person and can be known and spoken to. He came to us when we gave control of our lives to Jesus.
* His job is to help us understand more about Jesus, and to give us the power to do the things that Jesus wants us to do.
* We need to experience the presence of the Holy Spirit in our life each day. Many Christians use a prayer like this: 'Holy Spirit, please fill me today with your presence and power. Help me to know what Jesus wants of me, and help me to do it.'

Using this prayer every day will make a very big difference to our experience of God.

Must I become a missionary in Japan?

When we give control of our lives to Jesus, we automatically become missionaries. We have the truth about God in our hearts, and as that truth changes us others are going to notice, and we will want to tell them about God.

God might call us to any part of the world to live out this truth and to share it, but in my experience he first of all expects us to be missionaries for him where we are. This means:

Home and family

For most of us, the work starts very close to home. Do our wife and children know about God? Is the home honouring to him? Is the family getting enough love, enough time together? Sometimes we're very concerned about unbelievers in other lands, but ignore the unbelievers that we live with every day of our life. God would never behave like this—so how can we?

Friends and colleagues

Most of us have many friends and work colleagues who don't believe in God. We're perfectly placed to begin to help them understand what it means to have faith in God. It isn't going to be easy, and it isn't going to be quick. But we are there, and we have a job to do. Are you ready to be a missionary in your place of work?

Our community

Who will tell our community about God if we don't do it? Of course we're not doing it alone—there are other believers with us, but there aren't a lot of us, and we all need to pull our weight if our community is to become a place where Jesus is known and honoured.

Our church

Churches are supposed to send missionaries out, but some of them need missionaries sent to them, to revive faith in the church and to rekindle a love for God. Before we rush off to churches in Japan, there may be churches much nearer home that need us.

God certainly does call men to work in all parts of the world, and he might well call you. But first you have to serve an apprenticeship much nearer home. Are you ready and willing to hear his call?

How can I get on with that lot at the church?

Men often feel uncomfortable in church. The books, the hymns, the singing, standing and sitting—there are so many opportunities to make mistakes and feel embarrassed. Then there are the people, who are not exactly the friends we would have chosen—not to mention the minister!

Despite this, if we have given control of our life to Jesus, then we need that lot at the church and they need us. We're in it together, learning from God and teaching and helping each other along.

So if you are struggling with the idea of church, let me suggest that you:

Persevere

Don't give up because you find the church difficult. Sometimes it takes time to get used to church, and it takes time to build friendships. Pray and stick at it for a bit longer.

Join a small group

In these smaller groups—perhaps a men's group or home group—you can get to know people, and as friendships grow, so church doesn't seem so daunting.

Find the right church

If things really don't work out, perhaps you've joined the wrong church. We tend to go to the church that our parents took us to, but we need to look around to find the place where we are comfortable and where we feel welcome. It's better to look around than to give up altogether.

Be clear about the importance

We cannot hope to survive as a Christian apart from a church. Not only are we outside God's will, we will not be able to stand the strains and pressures. The perfect church doesn't exist, but somewhere there is a place for you.

The Christian Man

by Jim Smith

Can a man express his masculinity and still be a faithful Christian in today's secular world?

Jim Smith celebrates the enjoyment of being a man under God. He points to those areas which need particular attention if we are to be men of God – not least our sex lives, our family, our work (paid or otherwise) and our witness.

Men – and women too – will find here practical help and inspiration as they seek to work out their particular roles in today's pressured society.

Jim Smith is an evangelist with the Church Pastoral Aid Society. He is married to Mary, and they have four sons.

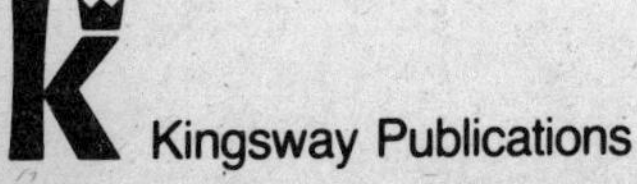

My God is Real

by David Watson

If the things Christ said are not true, then the sooner we throw this Christianity into a funeral pyre the better. . . .

On the other hand, if Christ's teaching is the truth, the position is very different. There may need to be radical changes in our lives, a new life altogether. What is necessary is that we should know what real Christianity is all about: and that is the purpose of this book.

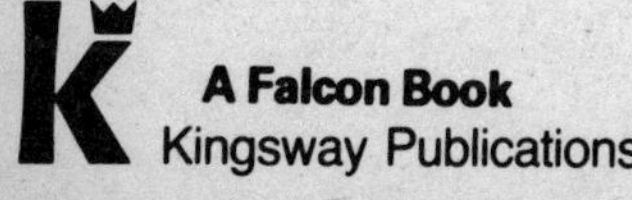

Foolish to be Wise

by Roy Peacock

As a scientist, Roy Peacock had a mind trained for meticulous observation. His understanding of the world seemed watertight.

But his growing cynicism about the world of the supernatural did not go unchallenged. Through a series of meetings with Christians of simple but vital faith, the foundations of his thinking and way of life were to be radically shaken.

The events that followed are related here in a way that is both lucid and gripping. Through it all we see that it is not necessary to jettison a passion for truth in order to encounter the God of the Bible, but that false prejudices must die if we are to walk by faith and know God's presence in our lives today.

PROFESSOR ROY PEACOCK has been on the faculty of two postgraduate universities and is the author of many scientific papers. He has been at the forefront of research in aeronautical engineering, and has lectured in many countries by government invitation.

Kingsway Publications